Praise for *Not Exactly Love: A Memoir*

"Breaking the silence about the c̶o̶n̶ relationships is the most power̶f̶ ̶, or
perpetrator—can take. Bravo t

— ̶o̶r of the

Ne ̶ ̶s̶t seller, *Crazy Love*

"Betty Hafner eloquently writes about being in an abusive relationship . . . A powerful example of how people can gather the courage
and insight to create a better life."

> **—Rosalind Wiseman**, Creating Cultures of Dignity, author of the
> *New York Times* best seller, *Queen Bees and Wannabes*

"Why do women stay—and how do they gain the courage to leave?
Betty Hafner's memoir is both a courageous portrait of a woman and
her will, and a moving guide for women who are also dealing with
the horrors of domestic violence. Her story will resonate with some
and give spirit to others, and is an indelible document for readers and
feminists everywhere."

> **—Lizzie Skurnick**, author of *Shelf Discovery*

"Hafner's deft prose puts the reader inside the story, revealing in inti-
mate detail the anguish of ongoing physical abuse, the slow building of a victim's agency, and finally, the redemptive power of boldly
taking back one's freedom."

> **—Robin Rinaldi**, author of *The Wild Oats Project*

"Betty Hafner's intelligence is on display throughout. She shares
such piercing insights that burst the bubble of attraction, enabling,
love and marriage, family repression, the complexity of domestic
entanglements—and her atmospheric elements do a wonderful job of
giving fullness to the scenes."

> **—Matthew Klam**, author of *Sam the Cat and Other Stories*

"For the literally millions of women who are physically abused and emotionally terrorized *Not Exactly Love* clearly explains the attachments, fears, and rationalizations that keep a woman trapped in a toxic relationship. Better yet, Hafner writes beautifully about how she took charge of her life and grew strong enough to break free. Both a gripping story and a manual for survivors."

—**Barbara Esstman**, author of *The Other Anna,*
Night Ride Home, and *Sure Thing*

"*Not Exactly Love* is a brave and honest account of a domestic violence victim's tense, unpredictable world. Illustrating many of the early warning signs that batterers typically display, it accurately describes the complex dynamics of an abusive relationship. Betty's story offers a raw, unflinching description of the tough choices and sacrifices survivors are often forced to make, but ends with an inspiring lesson on the cathartic power of letting go."

—**Lynn Fairweather**, MSW, Author of *Stop Signs: Recognizing,*
Avoiding, and Escaping Abusive Relationships

Not
Exactly
Love

Not Exactly Love

a memoir

Betty Hafner

SHE WRITES PRES

Published 2016
Printed in the United States of America
Print ISBN: 978-1-63152-149-2
E-ISBN: 978-1-63152-150-8
Library of Congress Control Number: 2016938339

For information, address:
She Writes Press
1563 Solano Ave #546
Berkeley, CA 94707

Cover design © Julie Metz, Ltd./metzdesign.com
Formatting by Kiran Spees

She Writes Press is a division of SparkPoint Studio, LLC.

To the memory of Lynn

Author's Note

I have changed the names of many but not all of the people and places in this book, and at times I have altered identifying details in order to preserve anonymity.

I cannot recall exact conversations from decades ago, but I have attempted in every instance to convey the underlying truth of the scene.

Part One

1.

Philadelphia, August 1970

On the sweltering afternoon of my wedding I took one last look in the bedroom mirror, happy to see no sweat rings showing. My fake eyelashes felt loose, so I pressed hard on my eyelids and scolded myself for not reading the directions. "Here goes nothing!" I said out loud to make myself smile.

At twenty-five I looked like a skinny teenager with my long sun-streaked hair, dangling earrings, and freckles. I wore no veil, no flowing gown, just a white dress with lace on the front and wide gaucho pants that had shocked my mother. The sleeves hid a new bruise on my arm, but that wasn't on my mind as I stood at the door.

I grabbed my bouquet—gardenias, not roses—and walked down the hall as if I were gliding down the aisle of a church filled with a hundred people, not just the ten who were waiting in the living room below. At the top of the stairs, I heard a rustling noise, probably Jack's youngest brother, and a loud "Shhhh!" I paused, took in a deep breath, and started down. But then it happened.

The heel of my satin pump clipped the carpeted edge and snapped off. My flowers flew up as I grabbed the banister and tumbled onto a step. No one could see me behind the wall, but they knew. I heard my mother gasp.

"I'm okay," I shouted and hobbled back up the stairs. In my childhood room, with a toy chest still holding stuffed animals, I stormed around in circles before throwing myself onto the bed. I clutched my pillow and hugged it like a life preserver.

The house was silent. No footsteps on the stairs. No voice calling, "How are you doing up there?" I could visualize our two families below, Jack's and mine. My mother—eyeing the group and worrying about the reactions of the family she'd met just minutes before and the minister who'd be waiting with his prayer book in hand. My father—hunched in his wingback chair, looking at his lap to avoid eye contact with Jack's parents as if they were uninvited foreigners not just my in-laws-to-be, on the couch with their four kids around them. Next to the minister would be Jack—pale and shaky with a hangover from barhopping with my sister's husband.

I was sure that every face downstairs must be registering confusion—*What's she doing up there?* Still, no one came. My family didn't have that instinct.

They're all waiting, I told myself. *You've got to go down.* Yet I didn't get up; I couldn't. My embarrassment was evaporating, making room for a chilling fear that trickled into my gut and worked its way up to my head. Maybe stumbling was a sign telling me I shouldn't marry Jack. I covered my eyes as though I could shut out the picture of his fist coming toward me.

I didn't want to choose between pretending he hadn't hit me and telling people what he had done. That choice was terrifying. My heart raced. *Do something, do something,* each beat said, *do something.*

"Everyone's expecting me down now," I whispered. "I should go." So I took off my shoes and flung the broken one into the trash. I grabbed my flowers and pinched off a broken stem. Taking a noisy breath, I stood up tall and walked barefoot past the mirror without a glance. I relaxed as I descended; the decision was made. I would do what everyone expected me to. The other option was unthinkable.

I passed the broken heel on a step and strode to my spot on Jack's left. It was there that I promised "before Man and God" that I would stay with him forever.

2.

One year earlier, on the morning after Labor Day in '69, I made my bed, chomped down a bowl of cereal, and walked the dog before driving to school for the opening-day faculty meeting. It was the start of my fourth year teaching French at Lincoln Jr. High on the south shore of Long Island. Walking into the noisy cafeteria, I looked around for other foreign language teachers. Each department was like a club, maybe even a gang, staking out its territory in preparation for turf battles and money fights later on. The only exception in the room was a couple who'd been having an affair for three years. In their case, Industrial Arts and Math merged at a table in the back, but I was sure that finding love at school would never happen to me. I winced remembering how two years earlier I had harbored a crush for months on a handsome, attentive new English teacher who, as it turned out, lived with a boyfriend named Steve.

I found a seat at the table where my language buddies were deep into small talk.

"Here we go again!"

"Have a good summer?"

"Yeah, great but way too short." We said the same things every year.

Our fleshy and flamboyant chairman, Freddie Flores, was making conversation with his sidekick Allen Hanks, a gaunt, effeminate chain-smoker who could deliver outrageously witty comebacks to even the freshest ninth grader. Freddie made his points with a dramatic wave of his hand; Allen countered with a well-placed puff of smoke. Nearby were Angela and Ellen, our two young Spanish teachers, one a blonde Italian and the other a well coiffed Jewish woman, both with strong Brooklyn accents. They were all as entertaining to me as TV. I had moved to New York for the people. As I saw it, people in New York were more interesting, more colorful than people in Pennsylvania. No study proved it; they just were.

Those two women ("the newlyweds," I called them) were as close as I got to role models. They talked incessantly about dinners they cooked for their husbands, furniture they ordered, and family celebrations they hosted seemingly every weekend. We all knew they were just putting in time at work before having children. I hung on every word of their conversations—I can still hear Angela say with eyes heavenward, "Oh, I just *love* the smell of fresh garlic on my fingers." With houses and husbands, and before long babies, they were on the other side of the great divide, and I was their devoted pupil.

There I sat amid the clamor of one hundred voices waiting for another year to begin, as single as a person could be. It was one month before my twenty-fifth birthday and not a boyfriend in sight. I had a roommate and a dog while my friends from school were coupling up like rabbits. In July I'd finished a graduate program in French Lit at Hunter and gotten my permanent teaching certificate. I'd been sure I would meet men in grad school. Magical thinking, that was, as if cute, eligible guys would be sitting alongside me in French Tragedies of the Seventeenth Century. It was that summer the Beach Boys had us all singing, "We could be married. Then we'd be happy. Wouldn't it be nice?"

To quiet us down for his "welcome back" talk that fall morning, the principal rapped on a cafeteria table. As I turned toward the podium, I caught a glimpse of a new face at the door, a guy who looked like a nineteen-year-old surfer with shaggy, sun-bleached hair marching in with his arms full of textbooks. He could have been mistaken for a student, but he strode in confidently, wearing the uniform of the male teachers—a collared shirt with a tie and khakis. The wrinkles in his shirt told me he didn't live with a mother, a wife, or an iron. With a blast of breath from his bottom lip, he blew wisps of hair out of his eyes, slammed his books down on the science table and dropped onto a chair.

Studying the stranger that morning, I had a powerful feeling that I knew him, not well, but that I had at least seen him before. I thought he might be one of the nameless freshmen boys who'd entered college at the start of my senior year, who showed signs of the cultural phenomenon blowing in. They'd be out in the work world that fall— those gawky kids with their unkempt hair hitting their collars and their bangs hiding their eyebrows.

That morning, I'm sure I didn't attract Jack's attention. Older by three years and sitting with the motley bunch of language teachers, in his eyes I must have been part of the lackluster wallpaper. To me, he stood out as if surrounded by an aura. *The only hippie in the room,* I thought.

Jack must have been experiencing culture shock in that fluorescent-lit room that smelled of Mr. Clean and brimming with middle-aged teachers, listening to administrators drone on about new referral forms. Later he would tell me that a month before, he'd been packed in with five hundred thousand bodies for a weekend on farmland in Woodstock, NY. He'd been tripping for days, he said, screwing strangers and rocking along with Creedence Clearwater, Janis Joplin, and the rest.

As other administrators made announcements, I studied our new faculty member. His pen ran out so he poked a neighbor and borrowed one. He scanned some of his reading material while the attendance officer spoke. His knees bounced together non-stop.

No, I decided, I had never actually seen him before. He just exuded the spirit of guys coming of age in the late '60's, and the life-force I saw in him was what I'd been looking for. I wanted some of his to rub off on me. It didn't occur to me I could find it in myself.

3.

On the first day of classes, I showed up in the cafeteria for fourth-period duty, the dreaded assignment I'd avoided for three years. Standing among the tables in the middle of the room was Jack, who'd be my partner for the year. He looked prepared—an authoritative frown on his face and a whistle around his neck. His long hair swung as he spun around to watch the room fill.

I had to shout when I introduced myself. That big shiny box of a room was vibrating with noise. The school had instituted a new policy—piping popular music into the cafeteria through the public address system to accompany the chicken croquettes and tuna casserole. So, added to the noise level that only junior-high-school kids are capable of making, rock music filled the air—The Zombies, The Fifth Dimension. To this day I can't listen to "Hey, Jude" without smelling hot dogs.

I looked at the sea of bobbing heads as I walked around the tables and felt a rush of pleasure. In two weeks I would be starting night classes for a Masters in School Counseling, and before long, I hoped, I'd be working with kids one-on-one.

From the middle of the room Jack got the kids' attention with a booming, "Yo. Qui–yet! Listen up, everyone. When I ask for your attention, I expect it . . . Got that? . . . Good."

Unlike me, he appeared to welcome his assignment. I'd been at the school for the past three years, and he was on the third day of his first job. Well, he said he did just graduate from a teachers' college, I reasoned, so maybe he's learned this stuff in Cafeteria Duty 101.

Tweeeet!! "Listen up, everyone," he shouted. A pause and then another Tweeeet!! His next announcement covered the routine for trays and trash.

Geez, I hoped we'd have some laughs, I thought, *but he's all business . . . He's pretty short. Maybe it's a Napoleon complex or something.*

And yes, I also thought . . . *he is cute, though.*

Every day I looked forward to fourth-period cafeteria duty, a fact that would have astounded any teacher who heard me say it. With second period free, I could stop in the faculty lounge and check my hair and lip gloss in the bathroom mirror. In the glare and noise of the packed cafeteria that September, Jack and I patrolled the tables and developed our routines. I stopped and talked to the kids who were sitting alone or looked uncomfortable. Jack sought out the troublemakers. There were always plenty of both.

"Where do you live?" Jack asked one day as we ambled along the tables.

"In a high-rise in Forest Hills," I said, excited that he'd asked a personal question. Hiding a smile, I said, "What about you?"

"Hey, you!" Jack shouted, turning abruptly from me. "Just where do you think you're going?" I watched a child-like seventh grader, probably looking for a bathroom, shrink even more as he slid back to his table. *Poor kid*, I thought. *Jack was a little harsh there.*

He spun back to me. "I live in Queens, too. Bayside."

"What did you do this weekend," he asked one Monday.

"My roommate Lynn and I saw a good movie Friday night," I said. *"My Night at Maud's."*

"Never heard of it. Is it playing around here?"

"No, we were in the city. It's French," and with my best Edith Piaf imitation I said, " *'Ma Nuit chez Maud'*. There's a theater for foreign movies near the Plaza. Lynn's a French teacher too so first we had dinner in a bistro in the 50's. *That* is our idea of an exciting night." I got him to smile.

He was waiting for more, so I said, "We did go into the Plaza afterwards for a Mai Tai at Trader Vic's," as if having a sugary cocktail at a tourist trap made it cooler. I failed to mention that on Sunday night we wound up at Lynn's parents' apartment in Flushing watching *The Ed Sullivan Show* with her four younger siblings.

"I go into the city a lot but never around Midtown," he said. "The Village, mostly."

The Village. It figures. Cool.

The piped-in music provided a soundtrack for our daily encounters; it made the job almost bearable. I kept the radio on whenever I was home or in the car, and I'd been dancing alone around my house since the early days of *American Bandstand*.

"Oh, listen. I love this song," I said to Jack about the tune playing on the PA system. "I heard it on the radio everyday the year I started here . . . 'Cherish is the word'. . . " I lip-synced along with The Association.

"What station do you listen to?"

"Usually WABC-AM and sometimes—"

"Oh, that terrible AM pop junk. You should listen to WNEW-FM."

So driving home I clicked to FM and moved the dial to his station. But at least once a day I clicked back over to AM to see if I could catch, "I Heard it Through the Grapevine."

When it came to our tastes, though, the most important thing in 1969, as the Vietnam War raged, was that we were both Doves. Had he or I been a Hawk, that revelation might have ended our story right then and there.

4.

I'd had boyfriends off and on in high school and college, but once I began teaching, my social life slipped into a coma. There were no available guys near my suburban apartment on an industrial street and not one on the faculty at my school. None. Lynn and I went into the city every weekend, nursing our drinks in smoke-filled, crowded uptown bars on First and Second Avenues. Guys would start up a conversation but would back away quickly when they found out we lived out on Long Island. "GU" was what they labeled us: Geographically Undesirable. As months went by, weekend bar-hopping lost its promise and became a chore. Our "pathetic" lives provided Lynn and me with enough comedic material to keep us up late in our beds laughing.

I basked in the attention I got from Jack during those forty-five minutes each day, so I accepted the new role he gave me—sounding board. When he wanted to talk, he sidled up next to me and spouted on and on about something that had driven him crazy that morning.

One day it was a simple request from a teacher sharing his room. "Can you believe it? She can't raise the damn blinds back up herself!"

Another day it started over a "stupid" school form. "Why do they need two frigging weeks to get a projector ready?"

He acts like everyone's out to get him, I thought. *He must be nervous about his first job.*

I was quick to make an excuse for him. He wasn't like my other guy friends, so I assumed he'd get over it. Standing there listening to his diatribes, though, made me uncomfortable. Minutes ticked by as we stood in one spot monitoring the huge room. The number one rule of cafeteria duty was to circulate at all times so the students felt our presence. But he stood and rambled on loudly with kids in earshot. I worried we weren't doing what we were supposed to.

One day during a break in his story, I walked away to check on kids at a table by the sunny windows.

"Hey, where are you going?" he said with a hint of alarm in his voice.

"I'm going over there to keep an eye on those ninth graders. Sabatino looks like he's hatching a plan."

"They're okay. Come back here," he said as if talking to an insubordinate student.

I stared at him for a few seconds. "No, I want to move around a little," I said and started walking away. Almost instantly, I felt him maneuvering up to my side.

"Who are you now?" he whispered, "The wild child?"

I didn't get his reference to The Doors song, but I did catch the attitude. "Hardly," I said, uncomfortable about what felt like a scolding.

"Good," he said in a tone that made the sun feel colder than I had hoped.

5.

On the last Friday of September, the school hosted a TGIF party at a pub to welcome the new teachers. Without any real buddies at school, I drove myself and walked into the packed room alone.

I could feel my stomach churning. The bar area had the cozy feel of an old English pub with a warm glow from red lampshades. The stools along the bar were filled with the serious drinkers who could order up "another one" easily without anyone noticing it was their fourth. They were also the biggest smokers, and the ashtrays were over-flowing with crushed stubs whose ashes formed trails back to empty glasses. The rest of the crowd was standing, packed in like lemmings on a cliff. I asked one of the old-timers at the bar to order me a gin and tonic. That gave me time to scan the room.

I looked around to see if my cafeteria-duty friend was there, very much hoping he hadn't brought a girlfriend he hadn't mentioned. Sipping my drink I made small talk with two men, married history teachers who had been looking for someone to flirt with. Among a small group by the far wall, I spotted the back of Jack's head. In a room full of crew cuts and bald spots, his long hair stood out. He was next to an art teacher I sometimes chatted with, and I inched my way toward them. Yet as I passed Jack's back he whipped around. Our eyes met for two seconds longer than normal, so I knew instantly we were going to get together, whatever that meant.

"Well, hello," he said.

"And hello to you," I said, clinking my glass against his raised beer, feeling suddenly celebratory.

"How's it going?"

"Great. You?"

"Better, now. Much, much better," he said as we inched away from the others. "Moon River" was playing in the background.

In 1969 it was not laughable to talk about your astrological sign, so we determined each other's right away—I, Libra (balance, stability), he, Capricorn (stamina, control)—and shared other bits of our personal stories. We found every chance we could to bump against each other while talking. We both knew this would happen.

I rummaged through my bag for my Kents.

"Ugh! What are you doing? You're not a smoker are you?"

"Yeah, sometimes. When I'm drinking or sitting around with coffee. You're not?"

"I hate smoking. It'll kill you."

"Okay. I don't need it now." I slipped the pack into my bag.

After a couple of drinks and a lot more bumping, he led me hand-in-hand out to the parking lot. I understand now if he hadn't had that boyish grin, those muscular hands I couldn't stop noticing, and if I hadn't been that incredibly horny, I might not have gone outside with him and started what we started. At work I'd seen his short fuse, his need to be in charge, but the gin and tonics washed away those thoughts, and I wanted his heat.

Outside we quickly decided whose apartment would be empty of roommates, and he followed me in his car back to mine. We kissed in the elevator all the way up to the sixteenth floor. Because we were the same height, our bodies fit together tightly. *As if we're made for each other,* I thought.

Inside the apartment we had an energetic, boozy make-out session on my couch. He quoted some far-out lines from an ancient philosopher or maybe a rock group I'd never heard of as his hands moved around my body. I couldn't make sense of half of what he was talking about, but I didn't care. *He's deep,* my compromised brain announced.

I was really into making out, but I said, "No, not now" when he wanted to have sex. One sober inch of my brain cautioned me that he was a guy who could be loud and bossy and a little offbeat. Before he left, he lifted the back of my sweater and lightly touched my back with his fingertips for a long time. I loved being touched that gentle way. I wanted more of him.

The next night in his apartment, when he slid down my panties, I said, "Yes, yes." A boyfriend. A lover. Maybe more. This is what I'd been waiting for, right?

I didn't have another cigarette for years.

6.

Jack's apartment became our hangout, since he had his own bedroom while I shared one with Lynn. I was impressed with what he had accomplished just three months out of college. Besides landing a job in a good school district in Nassau County, he had found an airy apartment on a main street in Queens; it was close enough to work in one direction and to Manhattan in the other. It was large enough to make rentals out of two extra bedrooms to help him with monthly payments, and he had found two roommates through an ad in the *Village Voice.*

Jack and his roommates spent most of their time in their own rooms. The two guys, both from Lubbock, Texas, were in a graduate psychology program in Manhattan. They were taking courses and undergoing their own therapy.

One night when they walked into the apartment with swollen red eyes, Jack looked up then quickly back down at the newspaper. A few minutes later he jumped up and called toward their closed doors. "Either of you guys want anything? Coffee? A beer?"

"Nope."

"No, thanks."

"Okay," Jack said, "You take care."

Sweet, I thought, happy to see he had a sensitive side.

Jack had also adopted two cats from a shelter. I was charmed by the names he'd given them—Isaac and Isabelle. It showed respect for them, as if they too were boarders, though Jack actually treated them more like visiting royalty.

One of the two was always with us, no matter what we were doing.

That was fine with me. During my childhood I had yearned for a cat, but my mother had a severe cat phobia and dashed away whenever a friendly neighborhood cat was around. We loved hearing the story of how when she was young, a neighborhood boy had thrown a cat at her, and it vomited across her chest.

Isaac, Jack's grey and white tabby, was an even-tempered, dependable guy. He and Jack were inseparable. Isabelle was a longhaired calico with a melancholic temperament. She watched over us from the back of a chair she'd claimed. We referred to her as the Nurse since she had a keen sense for knowing who most needed her warm, furry body next to them.

In our first weeks together, Jack and I rarely left his bedroom, passing through the living room only on our way to the kitchen for whatever nourishment we could drum up. His room was dominated by a disheveled double bed along one wall and along another, an elaborate stereo system with huge speakers on either side. Above the stereo he had taped a Woodstock poster from that August, one with a white dove sitting on the neck of a guitar. A small lamp on the bedside table had a red bulb in it. *Not much reading going on here,* I thought when I saw it. He had a lava lamp too, the first I'd ever seen. Jack had stopped smoking pot as soon as he started teaching, but those slow, sexy bubbles in the dark worked on both of us like a love drug.

Sex with Jack was vigorous, with heavy rock music pounding along with our bodies. He'd been a college wrestler and was strong and agile. My fingertips tingled as they slid along his rock-hard muscles. He smiled as he studied my body and told me my legs were the longest he'd ever had wrap around him. I felt adored.

For my birthday in October, Jack took me out to a popular steakhouse for a special treat. Sitting across from each other at a candlelit table with a glass of red wine and crusty bread, I felt like a celebrity. As a devotee of New York films from the '30s, it was easy for me to imagine us as sophisticates in a nightclub as we leaned in to whisper a funny observation to the other, he putting his hand gently on mine, me straightening his collar. The only thing missing was the cigarettes. We both ordered the same thing—steak rare, baked potato, and salad with blue cheese dressing—but I ended up giving him half of mine; he had the appetite of a scavenger on the savannah. I was finally in the relationship I'd yearned for.

7.

I knew and loved Manhattan by that time. Living in New York City had been a dream of mine since childhood, and right after college in the summer of '66, I had packed up my belongings, said goodbye to my family and left Philadelphia for New York. Lynn, my friend from college, and I took teaching jobs on Long Island. We had imagined ourselves living in the center of the universe—Manhattan—but one look at the classifieds showed us that city apartments were ridiculously out of reach for first-year teachers. We ended up in a one-bedroom rental in the family-friendly suburbs, along the south-shore line of the Long Island Railroad. I consoled myself with the fact that it was only a twenty-five-minute train ride into the city.

I had tramped around the city on most weekends with Lynn, a Manhattan expert. She'd gone to Hunter College High School and had made her way around New York City alone for years. She was a font of the kind of information I was interested in—which building Johnny Carson lived in, how you got into the audience of a TV show, and what to do if Warren Beatty was on the stool next to yours at the bar in Maxwell's Plum. (I had unsuccessfully tried to chat with him.)

Jack, a Long Islander from birth, became my guide to another part of the city. The Village was a special place then, sizzling with energy. The streets were packed with young people. The Doors and Santana streamed out of record stores. Head shops sold pipes and tubes and all sorts of unrecognizable vessels. Clothing shop displays were filled with bellbottom pants. The scent of marijuana wafted from open apartment windows. There was more facial hair, tie-dyed cloth, bare female skin, and men holding other men's hands than you could find anywhere else. Walking through those streets I'd find myself humming Buffalo Springfield's, "There's something happening here." In the short time since being with Jack, I had rocketed from the June Cleaver '60s of my youth straight into the Age of Aquarius.

Jack and I explored the city on weekends, usually ending up in the Village. We tried to pretend we weren't just a young couple from Long Island visiting the city. With my long hair, short skirts, and clanking earrings and Jack with his long sideburns, shaggy mane, and jeans, we could have passed for hippies. During my first week with him, I put my bra in the wash and didn't take it back out of the drawer for many years.

Back in Jack's apartment, it was mostly sex and music. Jack was crazy about both. He would crouch on the floor in front of his albums, thumbing through them until he found just the one he wanted.

"Here it is. Yes! You gotta listen to this," he said one night and daintily put the album on the turntable, advancing the needle to the right track. "Come here. Hey! Stop what you're doing." He pulled me down next to him. "Put you ear right next to the speaker. Great, right?" It was hard grading papers when one of Jack's favorites was playing.

"Bam. Bam. Bam, bam, bam!" he shouted in unison with Keith Moon's drum, tapping a pencil vigorously on the coffee table, eyes closed and head twisting wildly right and left. "Y'ever hear anything like The Who? Bam. Bam." *It's really neat the way he gets so stirred up about things,* I thought.

"I don't dance," he announced to me one day as if renouncing a religion, so The Supremes, The Temptations, and all the other albums I danced to alone around my apartment gathered dust back there. That was okay. Sex was an acceptable substitute. For a touch of mood music, though, one time I brought over a Johnny Mathis record, which he tossed aside like a Frisbee, not wanting it to soil his albums. At my insistence, he played Johnny's romantic crooning one time during sex instead of the throbbing rock album he favored, but I soon lost my taste for Johnny. Starry-eyed romance was not what my relationship with Jack was all about. The heavy beat of a drum was more in keeping with what we had.

As the weeks went by, we developed a school-night routine. While we ate dinner, we watched the nightly news together. In my childhood home the news was on after dinner every night. My parents sat quietly and watched while my sister and I looked at the paper or magazines. But Jack shouted at the set as if Walter Cronkite himself set American policy. "Just pull our fucking troops out of Vietnam!" or, when Cronkite reported what came out of Vice President Agnew's mouth, "Can't you shut that idiot up?" *Jack's smart . . . really into politics,* I thought. *Maybe I'd get angry too if I knew as much about what we're doing there.*

After dinner, we did lesson plans and graded papers side by side on the couch. I tried hard to ignore the snorts and moans as Jack waved his red pencil across quizzes, but his reactions were loud and, I could tell, meant to pull me into his world.

One night, he threw a handful of papers across the floor and slammed the pencil down.

"What's going on?" I said, taking in the mess he'd made.

"Ed picked a shitty textbook, is what." Jack didn't like much about his department chairman. "It pisses me off," he said. "How can you teach photosynthesis before the kids learn how cells get chemical energy?"

"Beats me."

"Is that supposed to be funny?" he snapped.

Yes, it was. But instead I said, "Don't you have the freedom to teach things in an order that makes sense to you?"

"The guy's all over me, looking at my plan book, asking what I'm doing—"

"He's a good guy, Jack. I'm sure he wants to be supportive."

"Great way to show it," he said, "peering into my classroom while I'm teaching . . . asking kids how it's going."

"The first year's really hard. It gets better, I promise," I said, but his eyes told me he was already in another world, inside his own head. When I said, "How about asking him to sit down with you?" I felt as if I were talking to the red pencil.

As I brushed my teeth that night, my gut still clenched, a sadness built in my chest. *If I were in my apartment tonight,* I thought, *Lynn and I would be on the couch laughing at Carol Burnett.*

8.

As the weather got colder that fall, I went back one Saturday to pick up winter clothes from my apartment. I felt a chill walking in, remembering the lonely person I had been there. The apartment was still dominated by a hand-me-down couch with two bricks under one of its corners where a leg should have been and a bare, scratched parquet floor where a rug should have been. I could see our two single beds lined up along the wall of the bedroom. A dumpy apartment hadn't mattered to us. It was only a way station until our "real life" started—the one with the husband, the house, and the kids.

When I set my purse on the table, I remembered how, during our first year of teaching, Lynn and I had taped a map of Western Europe on our dinette wall in preparation for our summer trip. Supposedly we were traveling to improve our language skills, but we were really only interested in romantic action. Every night at dinner we had discussed where we'd go with our Eurail passes. We dove into the planning as if it would save our lives. In a way, that's how it felt.

In London, I got my first miniskirt on Carnaby Street. In Portofino, I rode along the sea on the back of a handsome Italian's motorcycle. In Munich, I had a fling with Tom, an American soldier stationed nearby. In the *gemutlich* atmosphere of the *Hofbrauhaus,* after a huge mug of beer, I thought I'd met the love of my life. He and I had only our few days and nights in Bavaria though. Later that summer he visited me back in the apartment, where I discovered we had nothing to say to each other.

It was in the fall after we returned that Lynn and I got the dog, a puppy-mill pooch, at a pet shop. He was a West Highland White Terrier we christened Malcolm MacTavish. We decided whoever got the husband first ceded Malcolm to the other. My mother, apparently eager for a grandchild, knitted Malcolm a red sweater and matching tam.

The apartment that day felt empty with Lynn not there. She was going out a lot more, so Malcolm was the only one to greet me. He followed at my feet while I walked around taking in the place as if I hadn't seen it in a decade.

I sat on the couch with Malcolm's head on my lap and thought about how teaching French had been such fun for the first couple of years. After school each day Lynn and I had collapsed in the living room and talked for hours about nothing but our students. By October 1, we knew the first and last names of each other's troublemakers and the details of their inappropriate behaviors. There at home we would howl with laughter about an off-the-wall remark a kid had made or the outlandish thing he had done. (Yes, our troublemakers were all boys.) It was laughable how little our education courses had prepared us for the real thing.

In our first month as roommates, we had created a chart for our dinners, outlining who was responsible for shopping, cooking, and cleaning up. We didn't bother with Fridays and Saturdays because, of course, we would be in the city and soon, we were sure, out on dates with the guys we'd meet there. We would have never thought of just grabbing something to eat in front of TV. Each night the two of us sat at our little dinette table for our ritual. Having brought no cooking skills from home, I learned a lot of recipes that year, especially after we bought French cookbooks. Thanks to Julia Child's *Mastering the Art of French Cooking*, we would serve each other *coq au vin* and *boeuf bourguignon*. A rehearsal, that's what we staged each night, for the life we expected to lead in a year or two.

Malcolm pattered behind me, as I walked into the bedroom and surveyed its bare white walls and plastic venetian blinds clumsily covering the windows. The dog jumped up on the twin bed that I hadn't slept in for many weeks. It was carefully made with the same bedspread I had used in college. My dresser held my jewelry box and perfume bottles as it had in the dorm. The black-and-white poster of Paul Newman in *Hud* was still taped to our closet door. I slid it open, dug out my big suitcase, and emptied almost everything I owned into it.

I scanned the room one last time and could almost hear the laughter the walls had absorbed. Lynn and I had lain in our beds, laughing 'til we got tears about how doomed we appeared to be. How we spent weekends at my parents' house, looking for love in Philadelphia. How the way we dressed always made guys ask, "Are you girls teachers?" not stewardesses or secretaries that would have felt more like a compliment. How the two of us were heading toward life as spinster roommates in a run-down Victorian house with thirty-seven cats.

Sadness washed over me as I dragged my suitcase toward the door. When was the last time my stomach ached from laughing so hard? Jack was too edgy to listen to me talk about things in my life. When I told him about funny things that happened in my classes, he interrupted with outrage. "You shouldn't take that! I hope you sent the little jerk to the office." Soon I kept the stories to myself.

Malcolm trailed me into the kitchen, wagging his tail in anticipation of the treat he knew was coming. I opened the refrigerator instinctively and saw a stack of leftover boxes, reminding me how I missed going out to eat. I caught a glimpse of the little painting of a German beer mug I'd done that summer with a box of acrylics I had just bought. I'd been excited about picking up painting but hadn't touched them since I'd been with Jack. After I walked Malcolm, I pushed my stuffed suitcase out the door and shut it behind me.

I left behind my paints and the excitement of creating art. I left behind my family hand-me-downs and the memories they held. And I left behind the piece of my heart that held the joy that came from being with my best friend.

9.

When Jack wasn't looking, I studied his strong Irish looks—his blue eyes, freckled nose, and reddish brown hair. He had a face I'd immediately felt comfortable with, as if he were a cousin. But for a nice-looking guy, he paid little attention to his appearance. The first school night I stayed in his apartment, he asked me to match up a shirt and tie for him. He had me go shopping with him right away to pick out shirts and pants. One Saturday morning, he handed me a pair of scissors and asked me to trim his hair, since I had told him I'd given lots of friends perms and haircuts. A guy's hair was easy, so I did it from then on. I liked being so helpful, indispensible really.

How could I forget the hours I had spent in the last few years trying to conjure up a picture of the man I would marry? Lynn's teenage brother, who had a quintessential Brooklyn accent, once said to me, "I think you'll marry a guy with glasses." I was floored that this kid had given any thought to a match for me although I shouldn't have been, given how many conversations between Lynn and me he must have overheard. I mulled over his pronouncement again and again. Maybe I should be more open to men with glasses. Maybe I should specifically *look* for a man with glasses. I'd been obsessed with thoughts about finding a guy, as if I carried a little monkey on my shoulder, constantly nattering, "What about that guy?". . . "How about him over there?". . . "Maybe one of those two?" *I have a boyfriend now,* I thought, *so all that worrying's behind me. What a relief!*

That winter Jack took the job of assistant wrestling coach at the nearby high school because of his college experience. He threw himself into the position with the same energy and enthusiasm he'd had for doing a good job at teaching and even cafeteria duty. After practices, he gave me a rundown of what they had worked on that day. Whenever I asked what he meant by something he referred to—three-quarter nelson, granby—he gently demonstrated on me. Before long, I knew more than I'd ever dreamed I would about the sport and the boys on the team—their strengths, weaknesses, and fluctuating weights. It was fun to follow the team; a couple of the guys were my former students.

Our weekends started with Friday night wrestling meets. Jack went early with the team, and I drove over to the gyms where they were held. I liked being part of Jack's world and enjoyed watching the slow, calculated moves of the evenly matched opponents.

Sitting up in the bleachers, I followed Jack as much as I did the boys. The intensity I saw in him at home and at school was obvious here too. I also saw signs of his confidence, his composure, and his knowledge of the sport. I had never seen him teach a class, but I liked what I saw there in a gym. Talking slowly to the boy who was up next, hand on his shoulder, pat on his back. Afterwards, a broad smile at victory or whispered encouragement at defeat.

He was different with the head coach though. A cloud of mutual exasperation hovered above them when they were together. After the meet Jack let loose: "That was a dumb-shit move putting John in a higher weight class! He should never have sat Phil!" and on and on. His tirades washed away the pride I'd felt.

Besides being Regents-Scholarship smart and keeping up with news about politics and science, Jack was open to learning about all sorts of untraditional things. Spiritual things. Mystical things. Energies. Mantras. A lot of what he expounded on was new to me, but sometimes he said something that stayed with me for weeks. It gave me a new way of looking at life, and I was hungry for it.

When he put on an album by a group like Cream or Jefferson Airplane, he explained deeper meanings of the song lyrics even though he himself didn't drink much or take drugs. He could quote lines of Rumi years before I heard anyone else mention the name. He could sit cross-legged in a Lotus pose for a lot longer than most science teachers.

I was an avid learner then too, but what mainly held my interest, outside of the coursework I'd just started, was how people and their relationships worked. I read books I got out of the library like Mary McCarthy's *The Group* and John Updike's *Couples*. Jack owned books like *Yoga for Americans* and a second-hand copy of *Self-Hypnosis*. I was encouraged that he was looking for something that might bring him understanding and peace of mind.

I was grading papers in the living room one weekend afternoon, when I heard low humming noises coming from behind the closed door of Jack's bedroom. I opened it a crack to see what was going on. He sat in the middle of the room in a cross-legged pose with his arms propped on his knees and two fingers of each hand touching. One eye sprung open. He knew I would come in to check on him.

"Okay, so just exactly what are you doing?"

"Opening my chakras," he said as if whispering in church.

Where did he learn this stuff? It's not like he went to Berkeley. He'd spent the last four years at college in Upstate New York.

"What are your chakras?"

"They're the seven centers of energy in your body. Come here. I'll show you."

Jack moved his hand along my body, from between my legs slowly up across my abdomen along my chest to my forehead and pronounced the Sanskrit word he said would open each of them.

"So, naturally, the 'yam' I heard when I came in was for your pleasure chakra? The one for sexuality."

"You bet," he said with an impish laugh and pulled me down next to him on the rug. We slid out of our clothes and tossed them aside. He touched my breasts as he pulsed in and out. As he did, he kept his eyes locked on mine as no one had ever done before. I felt something powerful from him, something I didn't understand then—a longing that connected with something lodged deep inside me. I belonged with him, it told me.

Thinking back on those early months we spent together, I wouldn't say that I fell in love with Jack but rather felt connected to him. And I was in love with the feelings that were coming alive inside me now that I was with him. I was drawn to his slim muscular body and his playful smile, but also to his curiosity, his energy, and his passion for things, especially me. Being with him was something that satisfied by filling a cold spot inside. I felt my body loosen, soften, moisten. In the first weeks of our time together, he wrote me poems and signed them in his New Age-y way, "I am, Jack." He hugged me like I was the Christmas toy he had always longed for.

10.

Though people rarely talked about "living with" a boyfriend, I was one-hundred-percent "living with" Jack. Working at the same school all day and spending nights in his apartment, we were together all the time. The only time we weren't in the same place was on the two nights each week when I went to my graduate counseling courses out in Nassau County. But afterwards I drove back to his apartment in Queens in time to hop into bed with him. I still had my own apartment with Lynn, but since spending all my time with Jack, I had slept there just one time and only because I'd gotten food poisoning from a quickly-grabbed dinner after an evening class.

In the apartment Jack was underfoot like a hungry dog. Even when I was in the bathroom, he liked being right there with me. On mornings as I was briskly brushing my teeth before school, he often moved behind me cupping my breasts, rubbing them round and round. Once I teasingly said, "Enough already" using my best Brooklyn accent but that didn't stop him, so I turned and pretended to spit the bubbly mess in my mouth on him. When that didn't stop him, I wanted to spray it all over his face, but I didn't. I knew by then he wasn't the kind of guy to think that was funny. When I was on the john after morning coffee, he regularly pushed the door open, storming in to tell me about something that had pissed him off. I hated that; even animals seek privacy, but to him, whatever he was recounting was much more important than my protestations.

While Jack was at afternoon wrestling practices, I luxuriated in the time I had to myself. After he got back, most of our conversations centered on what had gone wrong during his school day. That was okay with me because it could be a way to help him deal with the people and school routines I knew well. But it didn't turn out that way. I'd give him my take on the situation that had disturbed him, then he'd give me his. Our takes were shockingly different.

I noticed that our conversations, especially late night ones, started to follow a pattern. When Jack started complaining about a write-up the principal Mr. Schantz had given him after a classroom observation, by the third sentence, he started talking faster. By the fifth sentence, he got louder and his eyes darted around. By the seventh sentence, he got angrier, because I wasn't agreeing that Leon Schantz was a flaming asshole. But then he caught himself drilling his points into me like a superior officer and he slowed down, moved closer, and softened his voice the way a mother might reason with a naughty toddler.

"You see," he said slowly, precisely, "the douche-bag just cannot understand what it's like running a lab." I could see his mind racing at top speed though. He rested his hand on my shoulder to emphasize a point and moved his body closer to mine. "Isn't that right?" he said calmly.

I knew what his touch meant—"Don't you dare move away from me." I couldn't anyway. By then my feet were blocks of ice.

At that point I was longing to hear him say, "Let's forget about it and just get to bed," but I didn't. When I turned my back to fold the bedspread, he said, "Now, you're *really* pissing me off!"

I never knew anyone so volcanic. Yet all the magazine articles said communication was what it was all about. Being honest, upfront. Putting it out there. Telling it like it is. *Maybe*, I thought, *this is something I have to get used to.*

I assured myself, *Yeah, he's passionate about things he doesn't like—upstate cops, the Vietnam War, phonies, Richard Nixon. But he's also passionate about things he* does *like—his cats, the Moody Blues, good sound systems,* Playboy *magazine* (articles as well as photos). I felt my passions growing too—for sex and animals and music and psychology. But passionate anger was not something I felt. I decided that his anger was just an expression of passion for life, and I had to accept him as he was. At that point, I wasn't even beginning to guess where it might go.

Jack was learning about me, too, in these late-night episodes, more than I ever understood. The most important thing he was learning was that I would take it. I took a lot. When he started to yell my eyes opened wide, transfixed, as if I didn't know what to do, which was, of course, the case. I listened, I empathized, I suggested, I excused, occasionally objected or apologized, but mostly advised and supported. I didn't walk away—his hand on my shoulder or not. I stood there, unwilling or, most likely, unable to move. I allowed Jack to make every point he wanted to make, again and again, with *this* supportive evidence, then *that* supportive evidence. We went back and forth for hours it seemed, but eventually I was the one who gave up.

Yes, he is being victimized, I would say. *Yes, he is right. Leon Schantz has terrible judgment about what should go on during a lab.* Then, and only then, could we turn out the light and get some sleep.

It struck me that my childhood home had not prepared me in any way to deal with Jack's outbursts of anger. My father was a painfully shy man who wanted nothing more than silence and solitude. He didn't demand it; he simply retreated. He was forty when he became a father and appeared bewildered by ending up in a household with three females. After dinner and the nightly news, he regularly went upstairs often retiring to the bathroom with the newspaper and sometimes, a cigar. We didn't see him for the rest of the evening.

When I told Jack how my childhood home was totally geared toward order and control, micromanaged by my mother, he winced as if I'd said torture had been routine. What he didn't stay around to hear was how she modeled caring and kindness for me.

My sister Doris, two years older, said once she always thought of us as twins. My mother was responsible for creating that illusion. She made a lot of our clothes and dressed the two of us identically. It's wistfully comical for me to look through the old family album (for she was a superb documentarian of our young lives) and see that my sister and I are, in every picture, no exaggeration, dressed in our matching homemade outfits with bows in our hair and our bangs cut short and perfectly straight. All this plus she was a full-time teacher—the only working mother on the block.

More importantly to our twin-ness was the fact my mother was adamant about treating us the same. She would utter no compliment or word of praise unless it started with, "You girls . . ." No word ever came from her mouth that would distinguish us one from the other. The positive aspect of that philosophy was that neither of us was ever anointed the annoying one, the shy one, or the selfish one. And neither of us was to ever think she was smarter, funnier, or prettier than her sister, or anyone else for that matter.

There was some conflict in our house, but it was in the form of bickering rather than shouting. My mother was a high school math teacher and was frazzled by the time she got home. She and my sister went at it throughout the next hours. These days someone might peg it as a control freak trying to parent a daughter with ADD. But to me it was my two closest family members quibbling and squawking at each other throughout the evenings. My mother stuttered when they got going, and I couldn't get out of the room fast enough. I learned early on I was better off by myself.

During my teen years, though, my mother and I had some of our own on-going battles.

I tried for a Jean Shrimpton look—"Get those bangs out of your eyes!"

I got my ears pierced—"That's just for gypsies!"

I shaved my legs—"You'll regret you ever started!"

Yet despite the everyday tussling, the home I came from was well ordered and characterized by fairness, often kindness, and no surprises.

11.

Jack was part of a big family that lived twenty minutes away from his apartment, and I was eager to get to know them; I had always wished for more brothers and sisters. He took me over a lot that winter as if he were showing me off.

As soon as we pulled up in front of their house, his mother and the four youngest kids usually swarmed out to greet us. His stay-at-home mom was a slight jitterbug who buzzed around us in excitement. She acted as if Jack were bringing her a friend. "What's our boy been up to?" she asked. "You guys seen any good movies?"

Little Timmy, who looked like an eight-year-old version of Jack, followed him closely, pummeling him with questions. "How long you gonna stay? What'd you have in that bag? Wanna see what I got in my room?"

Thirteen-year-old Brian stood back, but he couldn't hide his interest in what his big brother was up to and what this girl he'd brought home was like.

Eleven-year-old Diane studied me from head to toe as though I were on a page of *Seventeen* magazine. "Where'd you get those earrings? How old were you when you got your ears pierced? Wanna try a brownie I just made?"

Four-year-old Julie had been an infant when Jack went away to college. To her, he was still an intriguing stranger. She stuck close by my side, her hand latched onto mine.

Jack and I alternated lines when we talked about a kooky incident at school or laughed at each other's story about a silly thing the cats did. It was easy to feel like part of a settled couple when we were with them.

His father wasn't part of that energetic body. He nodded solemnly toward us when we walked in the door and went off to work around the house. He was a stocky builder with hands that revealed years of hard work. Jack didn't say much about his father, but I could sense a storm cloud above them. Jack behaved differently around him than around everyone else—slower, quieter, but somehow empowered.

During school days that winter, I sometimes saw Jack rush down the hall with his shirtsleeves rolled up and a scowl on his face. I avoided him if I could; I couldn't bear hearing who did what to him. I was relieved we didn't have the same lunch period so I was able to relax in the cafeteria with other teachers. In the middle of teaching a class, I occasionally caught sight of his sullen face at the door and froze on the spot. Thankfully he always moved on when he realized I wasn't available.

I noticed things, too, in the eyes of other teachers in school. None of my friends there teased me about my new boyfriend or quizzed me for details about where we went or what we did on weekends. They didn't bring up his name, and neither did I. I hated the uncomfortable looks I got from other teachers at the lunch table when someone innocently reported something the new science teacher had said or done.

"He was actually chest to chest with the kid," I heard a veteran math teacher say one day, "I thought I'd have to jump in and break them up." But when his buddy elbowed him and tilted his head toward me, he stopped talking and shoveled a spoonful of applesauce in his mouth. This was my boyfriend of five months they were talking about, so, afraid that others at my table might have heard too, I inspected my sandwich as if it were the most interesting sandwich in the world.

Many afternoons after practice, Jack walked into the apartment and launched into a rant about his bad day, just as someone else might walk in and pour himself a drink or flop down on a couch. How I wished I could have stopped the storm that blew in with him—just poured him a Seagram's on the rocks or something like they did in the movies. But he needed something more. He wasn't happy just to vent. He worked the story he told, manipulated it and before long, he would finally discover what he's been looking for—a way to blame me.

One afternoon as I was nursing a cup of tea in the living room, he slammed open the door, stomped in, and banged it shut. The room seemed to darken, so I said in a forced but cheerful voice, "Hi, Babes."

"You wouldn't believe what happened when J. D. mouthed off in my general science class." He threw his briefcase down on a chair as if punishing it.

"Try me." I smiled hoping to warm his mood.

"I marched that wise-ass right out of the room and took him down to Firth's office, and what do you think that bitch did?"

"I don't know." I hesitated, weighing the risks of an answer. "Did she ask for details?"

"She put her hand on the little shit's shoulder and looked me right in the eye and told me to get back up to my class, and didn't even let me get one fucking word of the story out before . . ." He tripped over his words as they tumbled out.

"Maybe she was going to call you down later."

"There you go, sticking up for that bitch, always siding with Administration." He spit the A-word out like a curse. "You never think I'm right. It's always, 'They know what they're doing' or 'Oh, the p-o-o-o-r kid.' You never see what I'm going through, how wrong they are. You automatically side with everyone else." He stared at me as if there were something else he wanted to say or maybe even do. A chill spread through me. He spun around though and stormed out of the room. I could relax only when I heard the bedroom door slam shut.

12.

A teacher's aide was on cafeteria duty that year with us. Rosa was a large woman with a shy smile and shoe-polish black hair. She was a conventional person—married with grown kids who'd gone through the schools. She said little but watched everything that went on in that room. Often as we wound through the tables, Rosa and I chatted about the kids or food or TV shows.

One afternoon we stopped talking to watch Jack at the door, gripping a girl's arm, pulling her back in, and scowling as they talked. He turned and shouted to us, "I need one of you here now."

"Hold on, Rosa. I'll go."

As I approached, I saw it was Anita, a tough ninth-grader, well known in the principal's office. "What's up?"

"Miss Princess here insists she can't wait 'til lunch is over to go to the girls' room."

"Sometimes that happens," I said to her, ignoring Jack's frown. "I'll go with you."

When she and I walked back in, Jack scurried up to my side to begin his diatribe. I could only guess what he considered my infractions. I was too easy on the kids, maybe. I didn't back him up. I made him look weak. I'm not sure, but that day I know I blamed myself. *I should have stuck up for him,* I thought. *I shouldn't have made light of it. I'm too much of a softie with the kids.*

Rosa had a role in our drama that year—like someone in a Greek tragedy who acts as a truth-teller, whispering words to the protagonist who is about to leap into the sea. But sadly the protagonist is driven by her demons and doesn't heed the advice. Rosa had startled me once when she uncharacteristically leaned in close to say, "Don't ever marry a man with a temper."

After that, "temper" became the word I used. *Jack really has a bad temper,* I told myself. *If only he could control his temper.* I used that word to explain his inability to deal with the fiery feeling that rose in his body and the need to relieve it by lashing out at someone close, like me.

I hated Jack's temper and was sure everything would be fine if he could get rid of it. I lived in the hope that I could be the one to help him stop feeling such anger and looking for reasons to turn it on me. The idea of breaking up with him wasn't anywhere in my mind. My heart goes out now to the young woman I was at twenty-five. Would other people be quicker to get up and go? To leave a passionate, engaged, loving man who fills up your life, just because he gets angry easily? I saw the part of him that was kindhearted and good, the man he could be, the man I wanted him to be. And I was sure I could make that happen.

All the same, I was becoming a person who smiled less, who talked less, who couldn't feel comfortable in her home. A person who carried an invisible radar detector instead of a heart, scanning the area Jack was in—the apartment, the car, the lunchroom—for the blips that indicated that trouble lay ahead. Sometimes I heard the alerts—angry outbursts or an object thrown—sometimes I spotted them— his motions much quicker than usual or his face knotted with fury—but mostly they came out of nowhere.

I imagine my young self at the time as teetering across a tightrope with arms spread wide, straining to catch each move toward imbalance. Each day she's in front of classes working to keep the kids' attention. Each night she's planning lessons and correcting quizzes. Twice a week she drives forty minutes to her courses. Outside of class, she pours over dense texts and spends hours in the library. But when she finishes all that, there is no rest. Instead there is Jack and his anger. Nothing she has ever seen or read or heard or thought has prepared her for what she faces each night. She and her detector are attuned to him at all times to make sure she doesn't slip.

13.

One afternoon that spring Jack walked into the apartment earlier than usual. He set down his briefcase, shook off his coat and kicked off his shoes. "Why are you rushing around like that?" he said as I headed into the kitchen.

"I need to get dinner together before I go to class. I'll leave you some of last night's stew." When I looked up at him, I saw the face of a ten-year-old staring at his birthday cake.

"I like you in that dress," he said. I looked down at my orange mini-dress with a white collar. "The top of you looks like a school-teacher," he said, "and the bottom of you looks hot." He sidled up to me and ran his hands down my sides.

"I'm thinking it's the bottom of it that's affecting you now."

"You got it." He wrapped his arm around me and kissed my neck just below my ear.

"Looks like you want to make me late," I said, bending my head back for more. I was starting to think, so what if I'm late?

"It's not my fault you're such a sexy woman."

Within seconds we were on the couch. My dress stayed on but my panties didn't.

I got to my class in enough time to get a seat up front and near the door. It was Mental Hygiene, a survey course covering a range of mental disorders. I was fascinated with what I was learning. I expected the professor to go over anxiety and phobias that night; it had been in our reading. Anxiety—that was something I could've lectured about.

Two years before meeting Jack I'd had my first anxiety attack. It was the most frightening thing I'd ever experienced. At the beginning of a class one day, I glanced down at my plan book to begin the lesson but it may as well have been blank. As I stared at it, a terrifying feeling came over me—not dizziness but separation, from everyone and everything in the room, as if I were in another dimension. Everything around me became loud—the silence, the cloudy light from the windows, the big box of the room where I stood. I didn't feel as if I inhabited a body; I existed only as fear. *Get me out of here*, my body screamed. But I was there. I had to stay there, right there in front of thirty-two pairs of eyes. And I had to return the next day and the following day and the day after that and every weekday after that from that point on, and since it was my career and the career of my mother before me, I had to stay there in that classroom for the rest of my life. Or so it seemed that day.

My body shook in time with my heartbeat as I stood in front of the group. I don't remember what I did for the rest of that period, other than running out for a drink at the water fountain, but it must have been okay since none of the students went running for the nurse.

I lived in fear of having another attack, but I kept going back to the classroom. I had to. I had never heard of an anxiety attack, and my doctor had no idea what was wrong with me. He prescribed the only medication he could think of then—a sedative that was no help. To deal with the fear of that dreadful feeling coming back, I would stand right near the door until I got involved in the action of teaching and forgot about myself. By the time Jack and I got together, the fear of the attacks had subsided, but I understood that they were sounding an alarm that something was wrong in my life. By moving toward a career in counseling, I was following my own preferred path. Yet for years after having anxiety attacks, I never felt completely sure-footed.

In the psychology class that night, I listened to the lecture and took notes, still feeling a juicy warm feeling below from the quickie we'd had. I thought about how Jack was annoyed that I'd insisted on heading to class afterwards, as if being with him were more important than going to my course. As the professor read from her notes, my heart beat faster and my hands chilled at what I was hearing. " . . . and in a person with borderline personality disorder," she said, "you find problems with anger and a frequent loss of temper . . . " I squirmed in my seat and put my hands under my thighs. "In times of stress, paranoia might present itself . . . " I rocked back and forth begging the motion to fling the thoughts out of my head. "Mood swings might be . . . " I crossed and uncrossed my legs.

I wanted to run out of the room but I couldn't let that happen again. I had to settle myself down. I took slow, deep breaths and rubbed my hands together for warmth. The teacher had moved on to obsessive-compulsive disorders. " . . . characterized by repetitive, ritualized behaviors that the person feels driven to perform." My body quieted down but instead of taking lots of notes that night, I scribbled a cube in my notebook again and again, just like I did in high school classes when I felt totally unprepared for an upcoming test.

That was not the only time I had the thought that Jack might have something more serious than just a temper, but that night I consoled myself with this: He can't be mentally disturbed. He's the oldest kid of a big family with younger brothers and sisters who all look up to him and beg him to come visit. He holds a good job and is a conscientious teacher who cares about his students; some of the girls even have crushes on him. Most of the time we have a nice life together. No, he's not troubled. He just gets angry easily. Too angry, too easily.

Not long after, as I was getting dinner one night, I watched him get so angry that he walked in increasingly smaller circles as he blasted out the story of someone's affront. "Honey, I hate to see you so upset," I said. That didn't get his attention but my next question did. "What about talking to a psychologist?"

He whipped his head toward me. "What do you mean by that?"

"Maybe he could help you find out why you get so angry." I slowed my words down as I watched his face tighten.

"Just what are you saying? You think I'm a sicko? You think I should be sent away or something?"

"God, no, Jack. I just thought it might help."

"Help? What would help would be you keeping your *stupid* ideas to yourself," he hissed as he stormed out of the room.

14.

The more courses I took the more eager I was to become a counselor. Later that spring I made the decision to quit my job in June so I could finish my Masters by the end of the following year. I could swing it financially because the lease on the apartment I shared with Lynn was up, and Jack would take care of the expenses for our place. I got an assistantship for the year that would pay for my full-time program in exchange for working in the Graduate Education department.

Remembering the unexpected events that led me to decide on counseling, I was sure I was on the right path. One afternoon in the spring of '68, the principal had called me to his office and asked if I would consider taking over the job of our female guidance counselor who was leaving at the end of the year. I couldn't believe he was serious; there were few female school counselors then, let alone one in her twenties. Just that week, when I'd been at a desk for my hall duty, a visitor to the school had mistaken me for a student.

I was thrilled he had considered me. I could easily imagine myself in an office working one-on-one with students—getting to know them better and helping them with things that were important to them. In college I had thought about becoming a guidance counselor but learned I'd need to teach for two years first, so I'd fulfilled that requirement. Right after the meeting I looked into the courses I needed for New York guidance certification but was crushed to learn I couldn't accept the job because it was a two-year program. But I'd never let go of the excitement that someday I might have a job that promised to be a perfect fit for me.

A tragic event in our school was the impetus for me finally acting. The mother of a boy I'd taught for two years had been killed at home in a break-in. It was a shock to the school; everyone was talking about the death of this PTA mom we all knew. Three days after hearing the news, we got word that the police had determined that the student's father had likely paid to have her killed.

I was in the teachers' lunchroom when a friend who'd heard it on the radio told me. I wrapped my sandwich back up. Who could eat? I couldn't stop picturing Bobby's face; the sparkle would be gone. This would change his life forever. Who would take care of him? I worried. What will he say to other kids when he comes back to school? Who'll help him get through this nightmare?

That is what I'd like to be doing, I thought. Helping him get through it, not introducing him to "*le subjonctif.*" Within a week, I enrolled in two evening guidance classes for the following semester.

When the school year came to an end, I walked away with more relief than sentimentality from the big brick building where I'd spent four years at my first real job. "I'm excited about trying something new," I told people. What I didn't say was, "I'm happy to put more space between Jack and me."

Jack had signed up for a summer course three evenings a week to begin his Master's program too, so the summer opened up in front of me as a fresh start. That June we moved our belongings into an apartment he'd found to rent near school. Unlike the bright second-floor apartment where we'd spent so much time together, it was dungeon-like. He was paying the rent so I went along with his pick—a cheap belowground apartment in an old house. He was proud of his decision. "I want to save for the future," he told me. The future? I hadn't been thinking about the future. I'd been focusing on getting through each day.

I couldn't believe we had to fit all of our belongings into the tight space that was to be our home. On the day we moved in,

Jack drove over to his parents' house to pick up things he'd stored there.

I went out to the driveway when I saw his car pull in. "Can I help?"

"No. I can do it myself." He opened the trunk and I had to chuckle at the tangled mess of fishing rods, buckets, and line he'd thrown in.

"It looks like you intend to do a little fishing this summer."

"Oh, yeah. Surf casting. At Jones Beach. Whenever I can," he said, unloading an armful with each bit of information.

Beach. That was a heavenly word to me. Childhood family trips to the New Jersey coast were beloved memories, and I'd spent two summers during college working on the boardwalk at the Jersey shore. The ocean and the waterways that surround New York City had been a big part of my draw to the area.

"I hope you don't have to get up before dawn to surf cast."

"No, no. We can go whenever we're up in the morning. Field 9. That's where it's best."

Ah, the beach. It will work its magic on us, I thought. And it did. Most mornings we got up and made the twenty-minute drive. We parked in the lot then, carting all our stuff, we lumbered across the deep sand to the water and tramped along the shoreline. It was quite a hike through the early morning bathers, but finally right before the impromptu gay beach, we stopped in the section where fishermen were allowed to stand and cast out beyond the breaking waves, hoping to catch stripers.

It was worth the trouble. All was forgiven and forgotten in that moist salty air with the waves splashing and gulls cawing in the blue sky above. Jack fished and became buddies with some of the others. I read and soaked up the sun or walked along the ocean collecting shells to decorate our apartment. Often I chatted with a woman who'd recently finished typing up a book that didn't sound very appealing to me—*The Godfather*. Most days before Jack and I went back to the car, we dove into the chilly waves and splashed around like kids.

Back in the apartment things were different. The place was soul crushing. It was simply a garage pretending to be an apartment. The front room, the size of one big car, was our kitchen, living room, and dining area. The back room, the size of a furnace and hot water heater, was our bedroom. Both were finished with paneling only slightly resembling wood. Our light came from one bay window across the front, exposing the cracked driveway. Just yards away was the roar of the southern end of the Cross Island Expressway. We regularly heard accidents. Sometimes, if they sounded close, Jack ran out to see if he could help.

One Friday night we heard the telltale screeching brakes and explosion of crashing metal. Jack sprung from the couch and tore out of the house without a word. With the place to myself, I decided to call my college roommate Carrie; it had been weeks since we'd talked. After fifteen minutes Jack came in, and when he noticed me, his face scrunched.

"Who are you talking to?" he said like a cop ready to arrest me for being on the phone.

I put my hand over the receiver. "Carrie," I said. "I just called her," though I'd really been talking to her for the whole time he was outside.

I turned back to the call while Jack got a beer from the refrigerator.

"When are you going to hang up?" he said loudly.

I put the receiver to my chest. "Soon. Just relax."

"It better be soon."

"Hang on a minute, Carrie," I said, covering the receiver. "I don't get a chance to talk to her much. You can't tell me how long I can talk to my friends. It's not your business."

Jack grabbed a magazine and headed for the bedroom.

"So anyway, where were we?" I said into the phone.

I listened to her answer with half an ear. I was too distracted and angry at his bossiness to stay on long after that. I emptied the dish rack and turned out the lights. I hoped it wouldn't turn into a big deal.

"What happened outside?" I called toward the closed bedroom door. He didn't answer, so I used the bathroom and then headed to the bedroom.

The door was open and Jack was standing there, blocking my way in.

"Slide over, please," I said as I pushed against him teasingly. He stood still and we stared at each other nose to nose.

"Come on, Jack. I want to get ready for bed." He didn't budge. An eternity passed while I tried to think what to do.

"This is not funny, Jack." I stepped back.

"I know . . . I'm dead serious," he said, still as a sentinel. "Don't think you can get away with talking to me like you just did," and as slowly as humanly possible, he slid away from the doorway.

15.

In July Jack and I signed up for a weeklong course at the Transcendental Meditation Center on Cordelia Street in the Village. Magazines had been covering this technique since The Beatles had met with the Maharishi Mahesh Yogi in '67. They'd become active proponents of TM, and other rock stars devotedly followed in their wake. When Jack suggested we take the TM course and begin the practice, I agreed right away. *This could be it,* I thought trustingly, *the thing that helps him.*

For the first session, we took the train into the city. To me it felt as if we were on an exciting, life-changing venture, yet Jack's face was tight and he said little; I was sad we were so out of sync. When we stepped inside the center, the atmosphere was still and serious, more so than I'd expected. We sat on metal chairs with blue padding in a small room alongside a handful of others. The teacher, Karen, who sat facing us, spoke as quietly and deliberately as a librarian. In the days that followed she told us how to prepare for meditation, how to quiet our minds, and during our third session we were each given our own mantras, which we were told to silently practice at home. The next day she asked if there were any questions.

Jack's hand shot up, startling me. "What if you're not sure you remember your mantra?" he said.

Karen raised her eyebrows. "We find that's not usually a problem." She paused. "Come here and whisper it to me." He obeyed.

Karen's eyes widened. "Oh, dear," she said, gently cupping his elbow and guiding him out of the room. Seconds later they returned.

I'm sure I chuckled to myself, but I'm also sure I never laughed about it with Jack. It strikes me as touching now. He wanted something so badly to calm his fires; it had to be a case of performance anxiety.

After our last lesson at the TM center we took the subway uptown to do some research for the graduate sociology course Jack was taking. He was working on a paper intended to show how the architecture of the urban environment affects its residents. We walked from 34th Street up to 50th, from river to river, sometimes with ice cream cones, sometimes with pretzels, calling out anything that struck us.

"Look at how they set that building far back from the curb so people can sit out along the fountain," I pointed out to him.

"Right. That's a good one. People can relax and interact."

"Over there . . . look how the shiny windows on that tall building reflect the sky," I said. "It's like a mirror making this street feel so much more open and airy."

Did the morning's long meditation open up something inside me? Maybe so.

We stopped at a drugstore to buy me a disposable camera for pictures of the examples we observed and a notebook for Jack. I acted as though we were collaborating on a documentary.

"Wait a minute, Jack. I want to get those two buildings. Look how the arched windows on the old one are much more pleasing than the rectangular ones on the next one."

"Yeah, yeah. That's good," he said. "Get a few pictures of it."

While I snapped photos, a young guy in jeans with suspenders came barreling toward us and clipped Jack's shoulder as he dashed past.

Jack stopped cold. "Did you see that guy?"

"Yea, what a jerk. I can't believe he didn't . . ."

"He's not going to get away with it," Jack said as he twisted around and pushed his way through the crowd. I dashed toward him and grabbed his arm.

"He was just a dumb kid. Please don't get so mad."

"You'd be an *idiot* not to get mad." He shook my hand off his arm.

"But you sound like you could kill him."

"Who the fuck's side are you on anyway?"

"I'm not on his side. I just . . . " but he never heard me say, "don't like seeing you so upset," because he took off toward Penn Station. I lagged behind, hoping to get rid of the knot in my gut. We'd had such a good day, starting out in the Village, finishing the meditation course, and working on his project together. Then Jack's anger rose instantly, savagely.

I could almost see my dream of a new Jack vanish into the dirty Midtown air.

16.

"Dad and I are hoping you can come down," my mother said when she called later that July, "and bring your new boyfriend if you want."

My parents hadn't met Jack yet. I was sure they wouldn't go for him. During our first months together I had told my mother and sister I was "seeing someone" but little more than that. "A science teacher, biology mostly," I'd reported, "oldest of five children, grew up on Long Island." I kept the details of our relationship to myself, the beginning of a long, sad practice.

I had a clear picture of the kind of guy that would pass their initial inspection, and Jack had none of those qualities. They would welcome a well-mannered, conventional person and a churchgoer certainly, someone who might influence me in that direction. My sister Doris, a former elementary school teacher raising a two-year-old at the time, had scored big. Five years before, she had married Joe, an ex-Marine with a crew cut, a good job, and a baritone voice that fit right into their Baptist church's choir. My parents were so fond of Joe they had asked him to move in with them for the year before he married Doris to be closer to his work.

My mother had called that day to tell me that my uncle, aunt, and their four girls from Vienna—"the Virginia family" as we used to call them—were coming to visit and she was planning a mini-reunion.

"Sure," I said. "I haven't seen them for a couple of years. That'll be great." After we talked for a while, I hung up the phone with a thud. What a lie to say, "It'll be great." What if Jack got in one of his loud, combative states in front of them? He made instantaneous decisions about how comfortable he was with others and if he wasn't comfortable, it triggered in him a need to take over. He determined on the spot that someone, anyone—a neighbor, a friend or her husband—was against him and then disdain crept into his voice when he spoke to them. He excelled at coming up with remarks that started acids boiling in my gut.

Yet I wanted to drive to Philadelphia and see my family. I adored my aunt, uncle, and only first cousins, and I couldn't put off introducing Jack to my family any longer. He was a big part of my life now, and it was time. So I decided to take the risk—we'd both go. By then we'd been together for almost a year, but I didn't think of bringing up marriage. As eager as I had been to find a guy, what I had with Jack felt so different than any traditional courtship I had ever imagined.

"Why don't you just go down by yourself?" Jack said when I told him. "You don't need me." He must have sensed the potential for problems being in close quarters with my parents.

"I don't *need* you to come, Jack. I just think it's time you met my family."

"Where would we stay? In their house?" He looked like he was experiencing a stabbing pain. What little he'd heard about my childhood home must have sounded like life on another planet. My mother—the teacher, disciplinarian, and church choir member. My father—the meek civil servant, church deacon.

"We can go see my friend Paula and her husband. I bet we can stay there."

"Well, okay, because if your mother tried to put us in separate bedrooms, I'd—"

"She probably would, Jack, but I'll come up with something," I said, staggering under the weight of the two worlds I was balancing.

I was hopeful that Jack would get along with the Virginia family though. My aunt, a piano teacher, and my uncle, a government worker, were down-to-earth, warm people and most encouragingly lifelong Democrats. I loved visiting them and their four younger girls every summer in their rural home when we were kids. Doris and I did things down there we weren't allowed to do at home—competing in watermelon-seed spitting contests, taking off our tops outside in the 90-degree heat, and running around their yard barefoot, way after dark, catching lightening bugs.

On that hot summer day in Pennsylvania all the adults of the family sat in a large circle in my parents' backyard, the younger girls behind us giggling as they played with Hula Hoops. My flimsy aluminum chair wasn't sitting right on the ground in the yard. It kept wiggling back and forth.

It wasn't the chair's problem, though. It was my nerves that rattled me, firing up erratically because of what I was hearing Jack say. He brought up politics soon after the introductions. There was nothing he liked more than finding fault with Nixon.

"You can't believe a damn thing that guy says." Jack announced in a voice loud enough for the neighbors to hear.

"Well, now, I don't think that's—" my father tried to quietly slip in.

"But he's lied to us again and again." Jack kept going with examples. I rocked back and forth in my chair. My aunt and uncle were a politely assenting audience, but not my parents who were loyal, though not especially involved, Republicans.

The anti-Nixon diatribe went on and on. "How can that idiot possibly expect us to believe that invading Cambodia is going to end this horrific war?" Jack said. "He's creating a damn police state! Just ask the kids at Kent State."

Neither of my parents said another word. I watched my mother, thin-lipped and serious, busy herself with refreshments and my father fidget in his chair. It was worse than I had expected. I knew Jack well enough by then to recognize that their disapproval, even though it was unspoken, acted like a stimulant for him.

I was instinctively a "bleeding heart liberal," basically a peace-loving, social-justice Democrat, and I didn't think we should be waging war in Vietnam. Yet I couldn't add any intelligent supporting facts to my position in that circle. The only coherent thought I had about withdrawal was, "I want to get the hell out of here."

At the end of that summer day in Pennsylvania, I took a picture of the group. It shows a broad smile on all the Virginia faces. My sister and her husband are pleasantly preoccupied with their toddler. My mother and father look grim and distracted. Jack is standing tall and smiling as if on a podium accepting an Olympic medal.

17.

On a sizzling hot day later in July, Jack and I tramped through the sand back to the Field 9 parking lot. He was carrying his fishing box, a handful of rods, and the stinking bucket. I stumbled along behind him with two aluminum chairs, my straw bag, and our towels. I almost crashed into him when he stopped and swung around. I unsnarled the chairs and waited.

He shifted from one foot to the other though the sand wasn't especially hot. "How 'bout we get married next month," he said in a tone as if he were suggesting pizza for dinner.

I wasn't prepared to hear those words, but, as though a switch inside me were flipped, I said, "Okay."

Something had to be going on inside my head then, but I have no idea what it was. Maybe I had been waiting for this question. Maybe it appeared I had no option other than being with Jack. We had been together a year, and marriage was the next step. I understand now that his question put me in a spot where thinking about it deeply and with raw honesty would have been the right thing to do, but shining a light on our relationship scared me silent. So at the beach that day, I said okay to marriage as easily as I would have suggested mushrooms to top the pizza.

Jack certainly was not the husband I would have dreamed up as a girl. I couldn't have conceived then there were men who got so angry and loud. As a child, I remember wishing for a tall, dark-haired, good-looking man like William Holden and suspiciously like my daddy. As a teenager, if someone had asked about my ideal husband, I would have admitted then I didn't know what I would wanted, but rather that I knew what I *did not* want. Sadly, that would also have been someone like my father, a man whose shyness was so consuming that he was uncomfortable being alone in the same room with me.

Jack and I agreed that we wanted a wedding that was simple and quick. No attendants, only our two immediate families. My parents' living room was the logical choice for a venue—free and well kept—so I called home to pick a date with my mother.

"Jack and I are going to get married next month, and we'd like to do it at our house. Can you get Dr. Hargroves to perform the ceremony?"

Silence. Then she said, with what I caught as relief, "Dr. Hargroves is away in August."

"Okay, that's not a big deal. Let's get the minister who's substituting for him." I made sure the tone of my voice conveyed the message: I'm marrying Jack no matter what. She might have interpreted it as the strength of my conviction, but I think now it might have had more "it's-too-late-to-back-out" in it.

We agreed on a Saturday in late August and kept the conversation short. I didn't want to leave dead time to hear any reservations I knew she had about Jack. She probably wouldn't have said anything. She and I had a history of not talking about my love life.

With the wedding date set, I went to Macy's in Roosevelt Field Mall and bought my white dress, not from the gown department, but from a rack of reduced, bohemian-looking things. It was the first and only thing I tried on. It had a lacy V-neck top, silky sleeves, and a bottom that billowed out into wide gaucho pants. I smiled thinking of the look that would register on my mother's face when she saw it, but I thought it was cool and it was my wedding. At a nearby shoe store I bought white satin pumps with a three-inch heel, a nod to tradition.

With two days to get ready for the trip to Philadelphia, Jack and I stayed at the apartment that Wednesday rather than heading to the beach. He moved fitfully through our place, banging drawers open and shut, rustling through the newspapers that were strewn all over.

"What are you doing?" I asked from my spot at the kitchen sink.

"Looking for where you put my goddamn *Time* magazine," he shouted over his shoulder. I hadn't realized it had come yet, but he stomped into the bedroom before I could get the words out.

A minute later he came back into the room brandishing the magazine that had triggered his anger. I could see victory on his face as he accused me of hiding it (on his overflowing nightstand instead of leaving it under the pile of newspapers in the living room where he expected it to be). He started shouting even though we were standing inches apart.

"You don't care about my things," he spit out. "It's like you don't give a shit about me."

"That's ridiculous. I never laid eyes on it."

"You getting smart?" he said, slapping the magazine against his open palm, "Huh? Huh?"

"What's wrong with you?—" I said before I saw his face and stiffened. Hate was what I was looking at. Before I could move away, I felt an explosion where his fist smacked my shoulder. I stumbled.

"God, Jack. I can't believe you did that!" I stroked my burning arm. "How could you hit me?" I hadn't ever felt pain that sharp. My mind struggled to accept that he did that on purpose. A weight settled in my throat.

His face was pale and without emotion; he couldn't answer why. He backed into the bedroom. I stood in the middle of the room facing the closed bedroom door, my hand still covering the hot patch on my arm. Something big was happening inside me. I felt as if I were filling with air. As if the person I knew myself to be no longer existed.

How could that happen? I had never seen an adult hit another adult. How could I accept that someone I loved had punched me? *The* man I'm about to marry *has punched me? No one can know,* I thought. *It's too horrible.* I backed onto a chair and stared at the door as if I didn't know who or what might come out of it.

That can't happen again. That won't *happen again,* I insisted to the terrified girl inside. Minutes passed. I knew I would have to come up with something to explain what he'd just done so my heart would slow down. So I could move ahead with my packing for Philadelphia. So I could get married.

Getting married is a big deal, I told myself. I'd been doing stupid things all week. I left my keys in the car and knocked over my coffee. He'd been acting stressed out too. So, desperate for something to make this all go away, I grabbed at the easy answer from the air—*it has to be wedding jitters.*

I let out a big sigh. Yes, that was it. The wedding. Now I could move ahead with preparations. I stood up and went back into the kitchen to check the packing list I'd made. I crossed off "6 pairs pants" and "new nightie." Then I went to the closet to dig around for a plastic bag to tote my satin pumps in.

On Friday, the day before the ceremony, Jack and I drove down to my parents' house for a rehearsal with the minister. At the trial run that afternoon, he and Jack stood at the bottom of the staircase waiting for me to come down from my room. I practiced my slow descent into the living room, but as soon as I stepped over to Jack, I began to shake—visibly, dramatically. I didn't understand what was going on. I couldn't make it stop. My lips quivered so plainly I could barely form the words I was asked to repeat. The minister smiled with compassion. "Don't worry," he said, resting a hand on my shoulder, "Everything will be fine tomorrow."

Part 2

18.

My parents are long gone now, but I have from my mother's old photo album a snapshot of me with Jack and his family following the ceremony. No matter what my mother felt about me marrying Jack, she went along with it and most likely talked my father into accepting it too. She bought a vanilla wedding cake, two bottles of champagne, and ordered a bouquet of white gardenias for me and a boutonnière for Jack. She snapped the photo with her Brownie camera out in their sunny back yard. It takes place after the stumble on the stairs. After the loneliest minutes of my life in my room. After the five-minute ceremony, our kiss, the clapping. After a flood of relief had washed over me, and genuine happiness took over. After our champagne toast and the cutting of the cake. After his five year-old sister caught my bouquet.

My mother had asked us to pose before Jack's family drove back to Long Island. In the photo I'm sitting on a folding lawn chair, my bare toes sticking out, and Jack and his family are encircling me. It's taken from such a distance that each of our faces is as big as a grain of rice, but it's as close as we got to an official wedding photo.

I examine our faces now with a magnifier; Jack and I both look like teenagers. Peering closer at myself, I detect something that looks like relief. *It's done.* I'm smiling slightly and although the sleeves are covering the bruise on my arm, something in my look suggests somehow I was aware of its mark on me. On Jack's face, standing among his father, his mother, and the four other kids, I see pride. I notice he is the only one smiling directly into the lens.

On the back of the photo I see a note written in my mother's perfect handwriting: *The entire Brennan family. The children go into 1st grade, 5th grade, 7th grade, and 10th grade in Sept.* She wrote it as if labeling a picture of her grandchildren. I see that she understood what a big part of my life those kids would become. In the photo, they're all smiling broadly. We were eager—his mother, brothers, sisters, and I—to belong to each other.

Little Julie, with her long dark hair, is standing next to me, holding my white bouquet and touching the arm of my chair. She was four when I met her. People often took her for my daughter when we were out together; we looked so much alike. Diane, the blonde middle schooler, was an early-blooming drama queen. She's laughing in the photo as she tries to loosen her mother's hand from around her waist. Jack's mother Jean, with surprisingly neat, even curls, must have made a rare trip to the hairdresser's; she was usually too frazzled to care what she looked like. She was in her forties then, fifteen years younger than my mother.

Good-natured Timmy, with his shaggy bangs, looks amazingly like a miniature Jack. Quiet Brian, the high school sophomore-to-be with dark bangs hanging over his eyes, has a shy smile. At that time, he was a year or so away from the pull of heavy metal rock and marijuana. Jack's father, wearing the biggest smile I ever saw on him, has his arm around Brian as if pulling him back into the family.

When I look at that picture, I think of it as the day that rag-tag bunch of kids officially became My Family.

Jack went along with my suggestion of Montreal for our honeymoon. I saw it as the most exotic place we could drive to and looked forward to showing off my French. But packing up his car in my parents' driveway that day, Jack headed to the passenger side and said, "You have to drive. My head's killing me."

I recoiled as if he'd asked for a divorce; in those days a groom always drove his bride off into their future. "You've got to be kidding! You can't at least start us off?"

"No, I'm serious. I need to get some shut-eye quick."

"You're telling me you're too hungover to drive to our honeymoon?"

"You got it." He opened the car door and collapsed onto the seat.

A vise tightened around my head as I settled into the driver's seat. Jack put on sunglasses and leaned back. As I backed out, I waved good-bye to my family without looking at them. I couldn't bear to see the bewildered looks on their faces at our version of a honeymoon send-off.

While Jack slept, I drove and went over the day again and again. The memories I called up, however, started *after* the ceremony. The stumble became for me, from that day on, an embarrassing incident—one to push out of my head. Instead I smiled thinking of our families chatting politely to each other, as though it were the first and last time they'd see each other. The kids digging deep for their best behavior. Jack lifting his mother off the ground when they hugged. Everyone laughing at Joe's "Happy wife, Happy life" toast.

When I reached the rolling hills and fields of upstate New York, north of the City's suburban counties, Jack woke up with a start. His head swiveled from side to side. "Where are we?"

"We're a little north of Dutchess County, I think. I saw a sign back there for Albany . . . ninety miles or something."

"Look at you, goddamn it. You're going seventy-three miles an hour. You're asking for it."

Then I remembered. Jack had "a thing" about the cops in upstate New York. He swore that every police officer there was a fascist pig and was against anyone young from downstate, especially someone with hair covering his ears. He imagined that his dirty, grey Corvair was marked with a target on it. He was everything they hated, he said—a longhaired guy from Long Island, driving an old car with a peace sign decal on the rear window. He hadn't told me details of incidents he'd had with the police, but there must have been some half-remembered events from his Woodstock trip. Ironically, he felt that his civil rights were most likely to be ignored in the vicinity of the town of Liberty, NY. (I had found out how serious he was when I'd tried to make a joke about it months earlier.) Getting within fifty miles of Liberty made his blood boil. Every plain, dark, American-made car was a suspected "unmarked pig car."

"Okay, relax. I'll stay close to the speed limit, and they can't do anything."

A laugh thundered from his gut. He spit out the words, "Oh, don't be so naïve. You don't get it. They're after us."

That sounded paranoid and scary, and I didn't want to think where it could go. So I stayed quiet and slightly under the speed limit for the next hour. I don't think Jack realized that in a confrontation with the police, I would have been less afraid of what *they* would do and more afraid of what *he* would do.

We spent the first night of our honeymoon in the DeWitt Clinton Hotel in Albany, whose neon sign called out to me above the city skyline. I was weak and shaky by the time we ended up there from the long drive with one quick stop at a Howard Johnson's. Jack was dopey from having slept most of the way, so we trudged up to the room. It was hardly a suite fit for newlyweds—simply a room facing the parking lot with little more than a double bed. We dropped our bags on the floor by the door. No talking. No snuggling.

"I feel sick to my stomach," Jack said as he flopped on the bed face down. When I came back from brushing my teeth, I heard the muffled snorts of an uneasy sleep.

I slipped into the pink baby-doll nightie I'd bought for the occasion. The silky little negligee belonged in someone else's life or in a Doris Day movie. I elbowed him roughly off my side of the bed, crawled in, and hugged an extra pillow instead of my brand new husband.

The next morning's sun erased the memories. After a good night's sleep, Jack's hangover was gone, and he was energized enough for a quickie. We had a honeymoon to go to, so we jumped into the car and he drove the rest of the way up to Montreal in time for dinner.

It was a given at the time that on a honeymoon you screwed like crazy, went out when you needed food, and, for a little bit at least, enjoyed the views of the pretty place where you'd planted yourself. That was precisely what we did. We eventually left the room that next afternoon after a morning of lets-try-everything sex with a short break for a baguette and coffee. Stepping onto the cobblestones of Old Town Montreal and picking up bits of conversations in French, I felt transported to my pre-Jack life. I realized that in my year with Jack, I hadn't traveled more than two hours from Long Island. Shortly before meeting him, I had been to Montreal with Lynn where she and I hung out near the university for the week. *But my guy is a home-body,* I thought, *so we'll probably do fun things around home.*

There were plenty of restaurants to choose from in the neighbor-hood, but we found a small bistro near the hotel. For our first dinner we celebrated with a bottle of wine in the dark, candle-lit ambiance. It was so romantic we agreed to go back the following nights. The waiters smiled at us at the door, happy to see the cute, lovey-dovey couple come in again. I filled Jack up with my unfinished duck breast one night and sole meunière the next.

Womanly. That's how I felt in Montreal. Back in the room I had clipped my long hair to one side and pulled it onto one shoulder, in a way I'd never worn before. As we wandered through the sidewalk stalls filled with art and crafts, I picked up and admired watercolor sketches with my left hand so I could catch the light on the twisted gold wedding band we'd bought in the Village.

Did I give a moment's thought that week to his nasty wedding hangover, his scary fit about state troopers, and the most pitiful wedding night I would dare imagine? Did I relive my shock at the punch to my arm? My stumble on the stairs and my paralyzing second thoughts upstairs? No. Not once. Things will be different, I told myself, now that we're married.

My strongest memory of us strolling around the streets of Montreal that week is that I was always freezing. I had forgotten to take into account that late summer temperatures in Canada might not be appropriate for short shorts, halter tops, and mini skirts—my usual August wardrobe on Long Island. As we walked around Old Montreal with a biting breeze coming off the river, Jack put his arm tight around me for warmth, but also, I thought proudly, claiming me.

19.

That September as a graduate assistant I was assigned to an education professor who needed help typing up and editing a book he was writing—a text on psychological foundations of teaching. I was lucky. My fear had been that I'd be doing paperwork or filing everyday. But Dr. Burton—"call me Jim"—was a warm, talkative guy who welcomed my editing suggestions and spelling corrections. He even asked for my reactions to conclusions he'd drawn. After I typed up his newly drafted pages, I was free to spend time during the days doing my own coursework in the library. Three afternoons a week I went to my classes. I picked up the academic life quickly and breezed around campus as though I were a tenured professor.

That fall our place was no longer "the apartment"; it was "home." Going from being boyfriend/girlfriend to husband/wife brought up in me an unsettling awareness. Something felt off when he and I were there together at home, though he was restrained, even playful. I think now it was most likely the stirrings of a girl steeped in the domestic culture of her youth. Maybe the realization that I was in this relationship for the long haul and would be doing laundry, buying food, cooking it, cleaning, etc., etc. for forty, fifty, even sixty years was shocking to my system. As far as I knew men didn't know how to do things like that. Jack, cooking? I'd never seen him open a can of soup. Cleaning? He was blind to the way the place looked. So, as I had always done, I made food runs to the supermarket; worked alone in the kitchen before, during, and after the meal; and schlepped pillowcases full of clothes to the Laundromat. I can even pinpoint the moment when this realization bore its way into my consciousness.

It had been a long day of work and classes when I got home to find Jack sprawled out on the couch reading a magazine.

"What are we having for dinner?" he said without looking up.

"Good question. What are you making?" I purposely dropped my school pack loudly as he snorted at my retort.

"I'm starved," he said. "They had those horrible fish sticks at lunch."

"Frankly, I haven't thought about it. There's some chicken from a couple of days ago that's probably still good."

"Okay," he said, looking at his watch as if this delay would throw off his schedule.

I assembled a casserole from a recipe I thought I remembered from a Campbell soup ad. I put the raw chicken parts, rice, water, and mushroom soup in a pan and made a guess at how long to bake it.

At the table Jack said with his first bite, "This tastes great."

"It's okay," I said, but I was proud about coming up with this fancy dish. But as I took my last bite I felt a storm brewing in my gut. I couldn't sit there a second more for fear of exploding, and I tore into the bathroom. I was on the toilet and miserable. I messed it all up, I groaned. It must have been that fat-soaked rice with some bacteria thrown in. Maybe I poisoned us. When I finally went back out, Jack was sitting on the couch with his school bag and a pile of papers.

I went to the kitchen sink and stared at the greasy mess thinking I had lots of schoolwork to do too. A voice-over sounded in my head, like an intro to *The Twilight Zone*: "You will find yourself here each and every night for the rest of your life. He will eat, get up from the table, leave the kitchen, and relax, as did his father and his father's father. Never mind that you did all the work buying the food and making the meal and you now have diarrhea. You are your mother's child and your mother's mother's child, and you do what you are supposed to do. This is how it goes." It took me forever to wash and dry those filthy dishes that night.

The surprising thing now is how crystal clear that scene from decades ago still is. Something happened there at the sink: I was beginning to understand that the way I was raised to behave, the way I saw women around me behave, and the version of life I thought I wanted was not what I really wanted at all. I wanted something different, something bigger, something that didn't make me feel like a scullery maid. But I had been behaving as if I'd accepted it, so I decided that night to do what I was supposed to do—for the time being. From that day on, though, I paid a lot more attention to what the radical women's libbers I saw on TV were saying. Women around the country were feeling it too, but in those early years, alone in our kitchens, it was hard to feel the camaraderie.

20.

For our first Thanksgiving as a married couple, we went to Jack's parents' house for dinner with his family. The second we walked in I could hear shouting from the kitchen. Diane was helping her mother with the preparations. Her voice was as strong as a corporal's.

"No, stop! Not that much sage." From the sound of it she was supervising her mother making stuffing. "Come on. You gotta keep blending it. Scrape it off there." She was the star of her Home Ec. class that year.

In the kitchen Jean was spinning like a dervish, shooing away the younger kids who moved along the counters, grazing for nibbles. I offered to help out, and she looked like she might hug me when I took over the job of peeling potatoes. Jack Sr. periodically piped in from the living room, "Hold it down out there, for Chrissakes!"

Hours later we sat down to eat in the alcove off the kitchen at a table covered with a plastic tablecloth and set for the eight of us. We were elbow to elbow. Jack Sr., at the head of the table, was his usual crusty, dark presence. Jean sat next to him, allowing him to give her a running account of everything that was wrong with the meal. I sat next to Jack and the kids were in their regular places. Two bottles of beer were on the table for the men. The rest of us had juice or soda. I noticed that Jack was speaking in a slower, more measured way, almost like a son returning home from a year of reading the Classics at Oxford. I could tell he felt proud in his role of the oldest son, now a married man, and likely the head of his own family one day.

Everyone was talking at once. In this family, getting food was a competitive event.

"Leave me some white meat! You don't even like it, dummy."

"You're only supposed to take one roll, Timmy!"

"You're not getting seconds, asshole!"

Jack Sr. piped in, "You kids better watch your dirty mouths!"

As the meal ended, hands grabbed for the one remaining roll, the last clump of stuffing, and the mashed potatoes stuck to the side of the bowl. The chatter fired up again when dessert was served.

"Hey! I always get the smallest piece. That's not fair."

"My crust is missing. Somebody's gotta give me theirs."

"His piece is twice as big as mine!"

It struck me as we finished up how different it must have been at my family home that very day. The table would have been set with the good china and silverware on the delicate tablecloth that my mother had tatted as a young woman. Water, never wine, would be in the crystal goblets, though one whiskey sour per adult, before the meal, was permitted. At the table before taking the first bite, the group must have recited the German grace my mother said as a child. *"Komm, Herr Jesu . . ."*

Traditionally my mother got up at dawn to work on the meal, although she began the preparations days before—slicing bread into cubes for the stuffing, peeling potatoes to be soaked in water. If I had been home on the big day, I would have helped out that morning, maybe snapping the ends off string beans and definitely setting the table. I loved bringing in autumn leaves to decorate it.

My father always sat at the head of the table and carved the turkey. He relished that role and did a perfectly good job, although my mother would have directed him throughout the process from across the table.

"Now get the other leg.

"Cut more white meat . . . thinner yet.

"Don't put the wings there, for heavens sake."

The only laughter at the table during the meal would have come from the teasing remarks that Joe and my Aunt Helen tossed at each other. The real focus of attention throughout the meal would be Marcia, the first grandchild.

"You're such a good little eater."

"Oh, she loves the potatoes. Give her more."

"Here you go, sweetie. Does she like gravy?"

At the Brennan house after our dinner, I played endless rounds of War with little Julie. That gave me time to think about my new life. The day had an energy I liked. It was chaotic and loud, but the kids fought over who would sit next to me, my new mother-in-law was eager to please me, and Jack acted like a celebrity. I felt satisfied, happy. *These are my people now,* I thought. *I'll watch the kids grow up, marry, have kids of their own. We'll go through life together.*

21.

One night in early December I had an oral presentation on the WISC intelligence test to give in a class on tests and measurements.

I got back to the apartment after my talk, and as soon as I walked in Jack's head spun toward me and I could see his clenched jaw. A knot formed in my chest.

"Where the *hell* were you?"

"At my testing class, you know that." I wished I hadn't sounded like I was fourteen.

He looked at his watch. He was holding a roll of papers he'd probably been correcting. "Did you go some-p-l-a-c-e afterwards," he said, enunciating theatrically as he inched towards me.

"Of course not. He always lets us out at the last minute, 9:30. What's wrong?"

"Why the hell are you walking in here at eleven o'clock?"

"It's not even quarter of eleven, Jack, and it takes me forty minutes to drive home. Plus, I had my chart to schlep—Oh, why do I have to go through this!"

His voice notched up several decibels. "Because, I didn't know what the hell my wife was doing and why she wasn't here where she belonged." He took a heavy breath.

Belonged? The word landed hard on me but I let him go on, " . . . and I need help with a formal complaint I'm writing up about this shitty . . . "

My mind wandered. I could see the rest of the evening play out before my eyes—listening to the Problem of the Day. I could forget about sitting down with my feet up and watching Johnny Carson to decompress. *What the hell can I say that won't blow this up?*

"Oh, please, Jack. Let's talk about it tomorrow."

"Tomorrow?" he said as if he didn't understand the word. "Tomorrow? So your school's more important than me." He moved even closer. "I could be dying here and you wouldn't even notice."

"That's ridiculous, Jack. I had this big report to give that's half my grade and I'm . . ." I tried to back up, but I was pressed against the sofa.

"*Your* grades, *your* courses. That's the only thing *you* care about."

"Come on. That's not fair," I said as I registered a flash of white in front of me and a stinging sensation across my face.

"OW!" I screamed. "Don't hit me with your papers. They cut me." I covered my eye that was starting to tear. "I'm not going to help you if you do stuff like that to me."

"You're *not* going to help me?" He was screaming now, so close to my face I felt the hot blast of his breath. "What the fuck is this all about? You're '*not* going to *help* me.'" He stomped his foot on mine and pressed hard.

I whizzed through my options like an animal caught in a trap. Fear was somewhere, but cunning was what I needed. I could think of only one thing to get me out.

"All right, all right, Jack. I just want to go to bed soon," and, as if I were waving a white flag in the air, I asked, "what is this thing you're working on?" A cold stone formed in my heart. I couldn't believe how I was caving in. But are there really women out there who would have said, "If you ever fucking hit me again, you'll be sorry, 'cause I'm outta here for good"? I couldn't have said that then. It would have felt suicidal.

I listened to him tell his story; he was calm since I was focusing totally on him. We went back and forth for an hour, and I made suggestions that he liked. *This is how my life will be from now on,* I thought. I couldn't do whatever I wanted anytime he wanted me to do something else. A jolt that felt like an electric current went through me. Perhaps it was my feelings getting zapped.

I was learning what to do to survive. Hold back. Tamp down what was going on inside me. Don't dare challenge him or tell him what he's doing is wrong or that he is scaring me. It only made his anger grow. The sad truth is the most dangerous thing I could do was stick up for myself.

It might have been later that month when Jack lunged at me and pushed me into the table. Maybe it was January when he got so angry he slammed me against the front door and the handle clipped my hip. Maybe it was February or March when he walloped my arm with a book he was holding. I never knew when to expect these things he did. It varied depending on his demons and not what I did, as he fiercely claimed to shut me up when I tried to talk about it.

His outbursts came so quickly and unexpectedly that the part of me that carried self-awareness shut down. It had to. How could I live my life being aware of what was happening to me? I even gave his physical outbursts a bland label, "incidents." I had to find an inaccessible part of my mind where I could stash these incidents and make them go away. And I did. I kept them all to myself. I didn't tell a soul—not my family, not my friends. I hated thinking about what it would say about me and the man I picked to marry.

The incidents kept happening, but I went on with my life. A lonely, deadened version of my life.

22.

It was a black winter night outside, but inside the Brooklyn brownstone fluorescent lights flooded the room. I slid my hand along a wood bannister as I followed Jack down the carpeted stairs into a windowless underground space, fixed up as a meeting room. It was below freezing outside, but the air conditioner puffed away. I rubbed my hands together, glad I'd decided to wear sweatpants. Who knew what to wear to a group therapy all-night marathon?

In the months since I'd left Lincoln, Freddie the language chairman had taken Jack under his wing. Freddie was a single gay man who loved to talk food, shopping, and relationships. He'd gotten into the habit of sitting with Jack at lunch and helping him work through run-ins with other teachers and students. He told Jack one day that his therapy group was going to have a special all-night session. The purpose of the marathon, Freddie said, was to wear down the controls and defenses that we hide behind so we can be more real. I don't know what he promised, but to my surprise Jack said yes right away. It took two long phone calls from Freddie to convince me to go along with the idea. Freddie could be persuasive; he was aggressively articulate and never doubted what he said. I liked the therapy part of the deal. But Primal Scream Therapy? Yikes.

That night I surveyed the room or, "the pit" as I was beginning to think of it, where we'd be for the next fourteen hours. The brick walls were a dirty grey. Eight wooden chairs sat in a tight circle on the dark industrial carpet. Jack acted jumpy, but my spine felt like a steel rod.

"Looks like it's set up for an inquisition," he said soberly.

"I know. I wish we knew someone else here besides Freddie." My breaths were shallow as I took it all in. *Is there a bathroom? Is there a water fountain? Is there enough air in here for all of us?*

The pencil-thin man who greeted us introduced himself as Paul, the group facilitator and the one who'd set up the marathon. I assumed he was a licensed psychologist, but I learned later he had no credential; he had simply logged many years of therapy and had been part of a marathon once before. He had been seduced by Primal Scream Therapy, one of the unorthodox techniques that were cropping up to help us all get in touch with our deeply-hidden feelings, anger being the king of all feelings. I shuddered when Freddie first described it. He told us the session was planned to follow the recently published book, *The Primal Scream*, of psychologist Arthur Janov, who had treated John Lennon and Yoko Ono. They reportedly were a perfect couple, so with that nugget of information I was able to convince myself that something good might come out of it for Jack and me.

He and I took chairs next to each other. Paul began by going over the process. "The first few hours will resemble our regular sessions," he said, directing his words toward the regular members of the group. "Our interactions will still be affected by the mechanisms that we all use to suppress the painful feelings holding us back from understanding ourselves and growing. But as the night wears on," he said, "we'll find that these defenses, these stories we create to hide behind, will slip away, and we'll experience the authentic feelings of anger, hurt, and pain. We'll go back to our very beginning, to the moment of our birth." He suggested that if we worked hard, out would come the primal scream, and then, having come to terms with our deepest fears and banished our defenses, inner peace would follow, or something like that. My brain was too swamped to focus on his words.

We went around the circle introducing ourselves and talking

about issues that came up for us during the past week. Paul began. He talked about his struggles that week, every week apparently, as a writer who worked out of his home. He talked about his difficulty getting out of bed in the mornings, then how much he wanted to stay in pajamas, unshaven, throughout the morning, then how hard it was to leave the apartment and go get coffee. *How will I bear fourteen hours of this?*

Others spoke. When it was my turn, I talked about how Jim had been using me to type the manuscript for his book and how frustrating his indecipherable handwriting was. I didn't mention Jack's outburst at me while driving over. I didn't even have the nerve to mention his name. I imagined that's why Jack had made sure his leg was touching mine. Others followed me, documenting their daily woes.

Paul asked us then to tell the group about our early lives and the feelings we had experienced as a child. This time, as someone spoke, the others were looking for tears or gritted teeth or any precursor to rage. Freddie didn't have much trouble. When it was his turn he ranted about his mother's controlling ways, pounded his fists against the floor, and cried. Paul encouraged him to tell her directly. He shouted and wailed, but no scream transformed him into a self-actualized being. He was simply angry Freddie lying on the floor. Others followed. By then we were all sizing each other up, wondering who would be the first to burst out with a primal scream.

I was positive it wouldn't be me. I knew I'd disappointed the group by not getting angry when I talked about my family, by not screaming about my father's inattention, by not punching the pillow Paul supplied to represent a parent. All that came out was a feeble whimper, " . . . and he always stayed upstairs."

There wasn't a clock in the room but I knew we'd been there for hours.

Then it was Jack's turn. Expectations were high for him since he'd told us about his shitty week and had taken longer than everybody else talking about it. He began to talk about his home life, delivering his words carefully at first—"oldest of five children . . . father is a builder . . ."—but before long his voice jacked up, his face tightened and the words started spilling out. " . . . punched me and kicked me . . . mother just stood there . . . " The group was pleased to see him go back in time, and Paul jumped in. "Yes, yes. Go for it." Others joined in. "It's there! It's there." I couldn't breathe. I didn't expect a scream. I predicted an explosion.

"Ask your mother for help," Paul barked. "Beg her to make him stop hurting you!"

Out of the corner of my eye I saw Jack jump up, fists clenching his wood chair and then, in the slow motion that follows disbelief, I watched it coming right toward my face. It cracked against the side of my head and knocked me to the ground. For a moment I saw only black. Then looking up I saw the wide eyes and open mouths of the people stumbling toward me before I closed my eyes again and lost consciousness.

Freddie drove me to his apartment where I remember the warmth of a little bed with soft pillows and a white comforter. He brought me ice-cold cloths for my head and assured me that there was no blood. Maybe he asked me if I wanted to go to a hospital but if he had, I would have said no. Going out into the world would have only made it more real.

It felt like I'd ended up in another universe—in pain and lying in bed in an apartment I'd never seen, in the care of the man who used to be my boss. When he handed me a couple of white pills, I took them, not asking or caring what they were. All I wanted to do was sleep and so much the better if I didn't ever wake up again.

The next day when I was up, dressed, and eating a muffin at his kitchen counter, Freddie announced, "You can't go back home now. You've got to separate for a while."

"I don't know," I said to the air in front of me, shaking my head. I may have said, "We just got married!" because I know that's what I was thinking.

"You've got to take care of yourself," he said, "and stay away until you're sure you can be safe. "

Freddie's pronouncement stung me. It got me boiling. I was hopelessly unprepared for the truth as I let it settle in. *As if I can just get up and go! As if I can simply go someplace safe where Jack won't come get me! As if I have family nearby I can stay with! I'm taking a full load of courses. How can I possibly go someplace now?* Separation and divorce weren't anywhere in my thoughts then. Not one friend in my neighborhood or school or college had divorced parents. Sure, it happened sometimes, but as far as I knew, not to people like me.

That night as I was trying to get to sleep, I heard Freddie talking quietly to Jack on the phone. Freddie was mostly listening but sometimes I could make out what he was saying. "Jack, Jack, wait a minute . . . " Then he got quiet. "How do I know it won't . . . " I grabbed a pillow and held it over my ears.

The next day at breakfast Freddie told me the two of them had spoken for hours while I was sleeping. "Jack had it really tough when he was young. I didn't know. I shouldn't have . . . " Freddie said quietly. "It all came back to him. It was too much."

The shrill ring of the phone on the wall made me jump. Freddie answered it and handed it to me. "Okay?"

"Hi," I breathed into the phone. Jack made a sound and then sucked in a sob.

"I am so, so sorry. I didn't know what I was doing," he cried. "Please, please, say you'll come home."

I heard the words but said nothing. I let his tears and his words drop to the floor in front of me. I didn't have the energy to forgive or not forgive. All I knew was that it was time for me to leave Freddie's house, and I had nowhere else to go. I said only, "Okay," to Jack and hung up the phone. He was over within the hour to pick me up and take me back home.

That year, 1971, there wasn't a women's shelter anywhere in the country. I wouldn't have imagined such a thing. There were no orders of protection or restraining orders. People didn't talk about or write about abusive husbands. I had no idea how much things like this happened to other people. Remember, at the time Oprah Winfrey was still a teenager growing up in Tennessee.

When we got back to the apartment, I kept my distance from Jack. He busied himself to stay clear of me. I couldn't talk about the inconceivable thing that had happened at the marathon. I didn't have the stomach to form words to label what he had done to me. Gone was the sense that it was a "temper." I understood it was something deeper, much more overwhelming.

In order to live in our house side by side—eat our meals, do our work, sleep, have sex—I had to assure myself that what had happened, that horrifying *incident*, was brought on by the crazy idea of an all-night marathon—a once-in-a-lifetime occurrence that would never happen again. But mostly, what I remember after that long night in hell is the silence around it.

A line had been crossed. No, a canyon had been crossed; what he did was life threatening. Yet following the marathon, we had good days, even good weeks, and I could imagine that he was contrite, that we had turned a corner. Maybe, I thought, he was shocked by his horrible loss of control and was learning to manage it. Nothing he said validated these beliefs. I just found it comforting to carry them with me, so I didn't have to feel what began to tear up my insides when I remembered Freddie's suggestion—separation.

All I needed, though, was to hear a snarl in Jack's voice, sense a sharp move toward me, or see a steely look in his eyes, and a silent scream lodged itself in my throat. Gone was my half-baked notion that things were getting better.

I heard the voice of my mother following me. Exclamations from the litany that made up my moral education paraded across my consciousness—"Buck up and live with it," and the apropos, "You made your bed, now lie in it." Above all, "It's not anyone else's business."

23.

That spring Jack and I combed newspaper real estate sections looking at houses all over Long Island. I remember how happy that made us.

"Look here," Jack said one Sunday, jumping up from his chair to show me a picture in the real estate handout I'd gotten at the supermarket. The hopeful conversations we had about owning our own house loosened us both up, so I brought home every one I came across, even though we weren't ready to buy.

"This house looks perfect," he said. "See, that's the bay behind it."

"It's adorable," I said, studying it, "but look at the price, Jack. It's way more than the realtor said we could afford."

"I know, but it's exactly what I'd like." He closed the booklet and tossed it on the couch.

"Me, too, honey. I'm sure we'll find an affordable one we both love," I said, wishing it were true. I hated watching his face drop.

One day I got an idea I was sure he'd be interested in. "I've been thinking . . . you know if we lived someplace else, someplace along Long Island Sound in Connecticut, maybe it wouldn't cost as much as Nassau County. It's so pretty up there. Let's check it out."

Connecticut. There it was, an idea that I threw out to him like a mackerel to a seal, and he gobbled it up. A change. A fresh start. Good for both of us.

"We could live right on the water there," he said, his expression visibly softening.

"Oh definitely," I said. "We'll dock our boat by the house." We didn't actually own a boat then, but Jack had been buying handfuls of magazines about boats and poring over them. "The prices will be too high close to the city though. We'll have to look further east, beyond where the commuters live."

That morning I ran to my car for the pile of maps I stored there. I unfolded the Northeast US roadmap on the table and smoothed it out to display all of Connecticut.

"I bet these small towns are charming," I said, sliding my finger along the coastline. "Everybody probably knows everybody else. I'd like that."

"Look closer to Mystic," Jack said. Mystic was known for fishing.

"Let's not wait for job ads to show up in the *Times*," I said. "Let's work on resumes and send them to school districts near the towns we want to live in." I dug in my purse for a pencil and paper.

The Connecticut coast was right on the other side of Long Island Sound, but for me it became "the place where things would be different." In Connecticut, Jack doesn't yell. He wants to build a future, away from bad memories of his early family life. He has a job in a school where they respect him and give him carte blanche in the classroom. I get a counseling job in a good high school, and after work I explain some of the problems I helped kids with that day. Jack tells me about something silly one of his students did. He laughs more in Connecticut. He thinks I'm funny there too, and doesn't perceive dark meanings in my wisecracks.

Ah, Connecticut, viewed through the filmy lens of hope.

But Connecticut like the rest of the country was in a recession in 1971 and no jobs materialized for us. I folded the map back up before long and put it in my glove compartment where it stayed unused for years, and Jack and I stayed right where we were.

I'm certain I've held onto this memory for a simple but powerful reason: it reminds me how Jack and I saw the same future, and I took that as a guarantee that we were meant to share that future. When things were good, we talked about our ideas excitedly. We'd move out of the apartment and buy a house by the water someday, we said. We'd make a garden big enough to grow flowers and vegetables, we added. Then the kids would come—two, maybe three, we agreed. I could imagine us working together to build a good home, a good family, and a good life. Jack would be happier then. Things would be good, I convinced myself, in this pretend future.

One afternoon I set myself up at the table to organize notecards for a paper I was writing. Jack came in from the driveway where he'd been fiddling with his car and got a beer from the refrigerator. His quick, noisy actions put my nervous system on high alert. He had a certain rhythm to his movements before he blew up that my body registered before my mind did. *Something must have gone terribly wrong*, I thought. He'd been tinkering with the car longer than he wanted to. Probably he hadn't fixed whatever. He got upset if he couldn't do something he thought he should be able to do.

He glared at me and our eyes locked. I froze. That was all it took, maybe two seconds, for him to realize his power.

"Where's the fucking church key?"

"I don't know. I don't use it." I said as matter-of-factly as possible.

"So, if you don't use it, you don't give a shit."

"I didn't say that, Jack." I couldn't help myself from getting out of my chair to help him look. He came at me with open hands as if he were going to shake my shoulders. I hunched over and turned to get away but not fast enough. He gripped my left arm, yanking me close, and with an open hand he struck my face. I pressed my palm to my cheek and felt the heat as I watched him go back outside.

It wasn't shock that kept me silent. His abuse happened enough that it no longer had shock value. But I had learned the danger of speaking or acting. It was better for me to shrink, to recede, to take on the presence of a speck of dust. And there in my nothingness, I would not incite him, and there I could remind myself that I had made my bed, and now I had to lie in it.

The next day in the grad school office, as I told Jim about a correction I'd made, his gaze lingered a second too long below my right eye. I had forgotten that on the days after an *incident*, I had to take extra time in front of the mirror, fingering through my make-up for the stronger cover-up to mask the evidence. That was my way of controlling the situation so that others, along with me, could pretend that nothing bad was happening.

That weekend, we sat side by side on the couch sharing the Sunday paper. A Moody Blues album played in the background. Isabelle was purring away on my lap and Jack was gently stroking Isaac who was stretched out beside him. When he was with his cats I felt as if I were seeing his good heart. He loved them—touching them, talking to them, and brushing them until they were in a state of ecstasy. It struck me that it was easier for him to be the person he wanted to be with them.

Our little family, I thought; *we could have such a nice life. Maybe he could hear me now if I said something.* I waited until he finished reading an article and folded up the paper.

"Jack, we have so much together." He looked up waiting for me to say more. I noticed him glance at my cheek. "You need to talk to someone about your anger."

"No . . . Don't go there." He shifted in his seat. "I'm sorry. Okay?"

"Being sorry isn't enough. You need someone to help—"

"Look, I don't like where this is going . . . " He leapt up and threw down the paper. "That's not going to happen," he said and stormed out the front door.

I sat stroking the soft fur on the cat's back, no longer caring about what was in the paper, but unable to find the energy to get up and move into the day that would bring who-knew-what.

24.

The fall of '71 found me sitting at a desk in the fancy front office of a sportswear manufacturing company in Manhattan. Welcoming vendors. Answering phones. Taking messages. Practicing the crisp, professional manner I'd seen Ann Sothern use on her 1950s TV show when I was a girl.

That certainly wasn't where I'd expected to be. I'd received my degree, gotten New York counselor certification, and collected good references. Even though the recession was waning, school districts had cut back dramatically and guidance departments had been slashed.

"You gotta do something," Jack had said. "We barely have a down payment."

"I'll find something to tide us over," I promised. "In the city, probably. Maybe a temp job." I would have never said it aloud but the idea of doing something completely different in Manhattan sounded pretty cool.

I went on the kind of job hunt I thought I'd never again need to. A search where I went down each column in the "jobs available" section of the Sunday *New York Times* and read every single opening. There weren't that many.

I found a couple of ads in Manhattan with an ever-so-slight connection to education to check out. I also came across an ad where I saw my height and measurements described exactly in a search for a pattern maker's model at a sportswear company. Before I saw that, I didn't know that there was such a thing as a pattern maker in the clothing business who needed a model, nor that my measurements made me an exact size nine which was, at the time, the basis for all patterns. I got off the train at Penn Station the next day, right by the garment district, so I decided to follow up on that one first.

I never made it out of the office. All my measurements, even from the nape of my neck to my waist, were perfect, they said, so Snapdragon Sportswear hired me on the spot. The pattern maker would size all the new patterns to fit me. To feel physically "perfect" for a small-chested, late bloomer like me was a treat.

Acting as a receptionist was something I did only at lunchtime or when the regular "girl" was out of the building. It was usually quiet up front so I could read. The book I read at the time was the new, tell-all *The Sensuous Woman* by J. (I threw my notepad over it when someone walked in.) At home, Jack grilled me on what I was learning from J. so we could try it out at night. Good things came from that cheesy book. From then on in bed, Jack didn't turn over to sleep when he was satisfied. He finished me off however I wanted.

The pay as a model/receptionist was small, but I didn't do much work either. The pattern maker, Sam, needed me only when a new design was ready for production. I had time to walk around the floor, watch the designers sketch out ideas, and listen in as the salespeople got briefed on next season's offerings. I learned a lot too, going onto the factory floor to watch the Portuguese women working their machines and talking to a young guy who came in periodically to sell accessories. I was doing something I never thought I would do. I was a woman who worked at a company in Manhattan. I liked it. It left breathing space around me. I felt like a different person, like a person who might have some surprises inside her.

But in November, after only three months at the job, there was a sudden counseling opening at Heritage, a big high school out on the north shore of Long Island, and I landed exactly the kind of job I had worked toward. I left Snapdragon with only ten days' notice but took with me the refreshing notion that New York City was waiting for me if I ever wanted to come back.

25.

Getting this new job felt like winning the lottery. With a new life waiting for me, every weekday morning I got up eagerly. I climbed into my VW, melded onto the parkways, turned on WNEW-FM and let the rock music and a cup of coffee charge me up. I was going to be in my world for the next nine hours. Even though I'd be listening to kids' problems all day, I knew the relief on their faces when they left my office would make it all worthwhile.

That stubby car was my pumpkin chariot. It took me from my home to a place where I felt special. During my first weeks at the job, when a senior was telling me about trouble she was having with her mother, she reached into her handbag and pulled out a pack of Winstons. She noticed my widening eyes.

"Oh my God, I can't believe I did that," she said throwing them into her bag. "It felt like I was talking to a friend." I made a point of remembering all of my students' names in the first months there— 350 of them. I got busier each day.

I wanted the students to feel comfortable in my office, so instead of using the glaring ceiling light, I brought in a lamp that emanated a peachy glow. I covered a large portion of the cinderblock wall I faced with a colorful art nouveau poster. Philodendron leaves twisted around the pencil holder and phone on my desk. Homey, that's what it was. My other home.

The faculty was mostly young and the atmosphere in the teachers' room was lively. There were only a few old-timers mixed in with visionaries, hippies, intellectuals, and party animals. The school had been recently built for the two thousand students according to a new concept: open campus. Anytime students didn't have a class, they were allowed to congregate in a common area where entertainers performed and music played non-stop, all right outside the guidance suite. (I had lunch one day with singer Harry Chapin at the height of his popularity.) The only thing that prevented the common area from filling up like Times Square was the fact that students were also permitted to leave the school grounds anytime they didn't have a class. Students I worked with in the afternoons often brought in with them the unmistakable scent of marijuana, this being before administrators caught on to that scene. When I compared it to my days in Lincoln Jr. High, where women teachers weren't allowed to wear skirts showing our knees until '68, I felt like a time traveler.

One afternoon, walking into the house, still wound up from the energy of the school day, I noticed Jack in the kitchen.

"I'm so relieved," I yelled to him as I hung up my coat. "My boss is going to take care of the college application process that the old counselor started with my seniors. He wants me to ease into the job, handling only the sophomores and juniors. Boy, did I luck out. He's a really nice guy who—"

"Whoa. Slow down. Who is this guy?"

I was surprised he was so interested. "The chairman of the department, Evan Bradford, so anyway he—"

"Sounds like a fairy. Is he?"

"Geez, Jack. No. He was a college basketball star or something. He's a little older than I am. Why all these questions?"

"You're acting like a bitch in heat."

"Jack, that's awful!" I said, but I refused to get pulled down. "He's a friendly guy who must be very competent to be thirty-something and the chairman. He's like a Joe College, cheering on our team. He—"

"Is that supposed to mean you don't want to fuck him?"

"Come on, Jack. Can't I even talk about work without you getting . . . " I said to the back of his head.

The truth was, it was fun to be surrounded by young coworkers, and I guess it showed. I was eager to learn and eager to please. I filed that exchange in the same spot in my brain where I had filed his ridiculous accusations about me going after a guy in my master's study group—in the folder called Jack-gets-jealous-easily-so watch-out.

There was more tension in our sex life now that I was back working in a school full-time. Jack never liked hearing about how exhausted I felt, especially at bedtime. At work I was busy every moment. I posted my weekly schedule next to the office door so students could fill in their names on a free period. Sometimes a student would come by and write her name in tiny letters at the top of the "Lunch" space, and I knew that meant it was her only free period, and she intended to take only a teeny bit of time. But it never turned out that way. She might start out with, "I walked out of my house last night and my parents don't know where I'm staying," so I never cut it short to go have a sandwich.

The beginning of the marking periods was the most hectic. Most appointments were for changing classes. Some departments had gone wild with electives. Phys Ed was the worst. I'm sure I contributed to half a landfill with the paperwork involved in changing kids from Archery to Square Dance or European Handball to Yoga. Then in the middle of that crunch, a teacher dropped in to tell me that Marie hadn't come to class for twenty-three days, and no one had told her parents, so would I please inform them. Then Eddie stopped by to ask what he should do because his semester-long Independent Study project was due the next day, and he hadn't yet started it. Then the attendance officer brought me a new entrant who spoke only Chinese, and could I please work up a schedule for him and arrange something with each teacher concerning his individual needs. School was where

I was me: busy, happy, creative, productive me. When I went home each day, every cell in my body was ready for a nap.

In our early days together, my interest in sex matched Jack's, but on many school nights, now that I was getting up before six a.m. for a long commute, Jack's hands on my bare skin had an unwelcome feel. My interest had waned, and I had always assumed that Jack's would wane too over time. That assumption came from something a college boyfriend had once told me. As if reporting a scientific experiment, he said if you put a penny in a bottle each time you have sex in your first year of marriage and then take a penny out each time you have sex in the following years, you'll never empty the bottle of pennies. Maybe so in the days of pioneers and penny jars, but not in our house.

Jack's personal quest, though, was to allow no position known to the human species to be untried. He had added *The Joy of Sex*, with its quirky drawings, to our sexual book and periodical collection. *Penthouse* had joined *Playboy* in his magazine pile in our bedroom and, on many nights, he would read me the *Penthouse* "Forum" readers' questions seeking information about their troubling erotic situations.

Sex to me was something that should evolve from a shared look or a laugh, a touch or a hug that woke up a part of my body, and an energy passed between that drew us together. As touchy-feely as it sounds, that was my idea of how I'd have liked our sex to be. To Jack, sex had nothing to do with what was in the air between us. He didn't even have to be looking at me. We didn't have to be in good moods. Sex to Jack was something he was entitled to each night. To him it meant immediately fondling his favorite parts of my body, then directing my head towards his penis, then arranging my body in the position of his choosing, followed by a rapid thunder of thrusts.

So things didn't go well at bedtime on many workdays when all I wanted to do was sleep. His presumption was that if he pleaded his case and insisted it was my responsibility, suggested that possibly I had become "frigid" and kept at me long enough, he would get what he was entitled to. His arguments often began at 11:30 and lasted indefinitely. He always succeeded by wearing me down. Sleep deprivation is, after all, a form of torture.

26.

That spring when our bank accounts reached the magic number, allowing us to make a down payment on a house, Jack and I pored through the Sunday papers. We circled any houses in our price range on or near the water. We weighed the pros and cons of Nassau County versus Suffolk County. One, closer to the city, family, and friends and the other, further from the city but less expensive. What about the North Shore (not as bustling, more expensive) or South Shore (close to the ocean, more congested)? But when it came time to view houses, we saw only one. A realtor walked us through a neglected two-bedroom-one-bath Cape Cod on a small lot along a canal on the South Shore. After the showing, Jack and I agreed right there on the sidewalk out front, "This is it!"

Before we had the realtor write up the contract, Jack asked his father to go through the house with us as an experienced builder. Outside his father lingered by the crumbling dock, studying the water. We knew not to expect much talk or excitement. He nodded to Jack, so we put in a contract and got it for the asking price of $28,000.

In spite of my qualms about a house in the suburbs, we moved in. It felt so different than the suburbs I knew, with its canal in the backyard that eventually flowed into the ocean and then on to anywhere in the world. The house, along with the property, had been advertised as handyman special, and it was unquestionably a wreck. A large chunk of the backyard had slid into the canal over the years, so one of the first things we had to do was arrange for a new bulkhead to be built to reclaim our backyard from the bottom of the canal. When the marine construction workers came to build it, Jack directed them to dump the dirt and sand dug up from the deep onto the yard, so we could start with an unblemished canvas—a flat backyard made completely of dirty sand.

Yet when I looked at the house I saw the cozy cottage it could be. When Jack looked at it he saw it for the marina it could be. Within months he and his father each bought fishing boats, and the two crafts soon lined our brand new dock.

We saw a lot more of Jack's father now that his boat was docked out back. He greeted us with a nod and carried his toolbox and gear onto the boat. He stayed for the whole afternoon, puttering with this and that, but rarely spoke to us. I knew from the therapy marathon that he'd been abusive but Jack hadn't said more.

"What's up with your father?" I asked one evening after dinner. "You two don't talk much." Jack's face stiffened and his body stilled. He looked right through me, not saying a word, as though the answer would take a lifetime to tell. But then it came pouring out.

I learned that night that inside Jack was a boy who had lived in a house with a father who wrought whatever hell he felt inclined to on his wife and his oldest son. Jack was a boy whose beloved ham radio was thrown out the window and shattered, before getting a bloody beating for listening to it too long. Jack was a boy who escaped out the back door on a winter night, wearing only underpants, and crouched against the garage as his father came at him with a baseball bat. Jack was a boy who watched his father hold his mother's head over a toilet with a knife at her throat and cringed, unable to speak for fear of being next.

But as a strong and athletic teen, he fought back one night, and beat up his father. He didn't give me the details but said only that after that night things changed. He told me only those few stories about his father, but they were enough.

I loved the idea that being a married woman with a home meant being creative, skilled at fixing up, and decorating. Planting things and nurturing them. Having pets running around. Raising a bunch of kids. Loving these things and loving them out loud. These images made up my own version of the perfect life, not one of which I had gotten from my own upbringing. They were a big part of what had drawn me to Jack, whom I saw as a partner in creating this life that was bigger, richer, noisier, and more colorful than my family life had been.

The clapboard on the house was a dirty grey, so I decided to paint the entire outside green. The fact that I had never even painted a wall didn't stop me. Jack said it looked like a new house.

He announced one day that the backyard garden of our not-quite-quarter-acre plot would be totally organic. We shared the idea of overflowing gardens. I visualized beds brimming with showy flowers from spring through fall, then cut and in vases throughout the house. I imagined beds of peppers, beans, and vegetables of all types and juicy tomatoes with zucchini plants twisting in and around them. I poured over the Burpee and Spring Hill catalogs and became an expert on annuals and perennials that bloomed in full sun and rich soil in Zone 7.

Our first big project was to make our small kitchen into a cozy space we could use for cooking, eating, and working. We didn't have the cash for new appliances or flooring, so I cleaned them up as well as I could. There wasn't enough room for a table and chairs, so Jack got a huge, thick slab of butcher block, four wooden legs to hold it up, and two stools. It took up most of the kitchen and was hard to maneuver around it, but that didn't matter. It became the center of activity in the house.

I put up a big corkboard next to the wall phone for a calendar, reminders, and, maybe one day, for our kids' drawings. I painted the cabinets blue, and it was there at the old kitchen sink surrounded by those cabinets where I would spend scores of hours looking out at our yard and watching the canal rise and fall with the tide.

Jack worked on the backyard anytime he wasn't at school. One afternoon he rushed into the kitchen. "You're not going to believe what I just heard." His cheeks were bright pink and his eyelids were fluttering as if he were a five-year-old watching his first circus.

"We can make our garden completely out of mulch that's free at the County Waste Facility. They've got huge piles of decayed leaf compost."

Free dirt didn't excite me much, but I said. "That's great. Need me to help?"

"Are you kidding? It'll take the two of us at least three or four trips to load up all we need."

Off we went to the dump and, side by side, shoveled up carloads of composted leaves. At home we loaded the muck into fourteen black garbage bags, and we dragged them onto the front lawn, since the backyard was filled with tons of the railroad ties he'd ordered for edging. I'd do anything, put up with anything, I pledged, to see him this happy.

Jack became an organic-gardening expert by reading everything he could get his hands on. Rodale Press's *Organic Farming and Gardening* and *Prevention* assured him that they held the natural secrets to health and longevity. He imported worms and ladybugs. Our one-car garage evolved into the storage depot for bags of dried blood, bone meal, lime, and other substances that were, in reality, dried turds.

One of our two bedrooms was devoted to seedlings. We officially named it "the plant room." The greenery shared the space with two tropical fish tanks. That room was alive, always steamy, with tank filters bubbling and lights warming the wet soil day and night. Jack hovered over his seedlings like a mother over her newborn. All of their temperature, lighting, and moisture needs were met and, because of his all-encompassing research, they were even "talked-to." It was his world where he could control it all. When he was working in there, I liked to go in and warm him up, ask questions. He answered as if he were the patient teacher and I, the curious student. He surprised me at how much he knew about the needs of saltwater tropical fish and three-quarter-inch-high tomato plants. This was the man I loved.

It struck me that Jack was so energetically working on our house and property that he must have felt as though he was putting his family life behind him and starting anew. When our sandy backyard was finally covered with the raised gardens, he and I worked side by side planting them out. I loved digging in the dark, rich soil and firming the ground around the young flowering plants we had chosen. I had spent hours looking at the Sunset landscape books, learning how to arrange flowerbeds by color and height and season of bloom.

One cloudy summer day we were kneeling next to each other on the hard sand with hand tools scattered around. I grabbed a container of red nasturtiums to plant in front of the black-eyed Susans.

"What the hell are you doing?" he said. "The nasturtium goes in front of the tomatoes. Leave 'em there!"

"Okay, okay. Cool it."

He stood up brushing off his knees. "Why? We're just talking. People shouldn't hear us talking?"

"You're not talking, Jack. You're yelling."

He was hovering over me now. "Don't tell me what I'm doing! You know how important it is to have plants working together. You'd rather put chemicals all over the place and ruin our food?" His knee ground into my back. "Huh? Do you? Well, you're acting that way and I swear to God if you ruin this project that's taken me months—"

I stood up to make myself bigger. "Come on, Jack, relax. I can't remember *all* the organic rules." *Think of something, think of something,* I willed myself.

His face turned scarlet as he shouted, "Then you'd goddamn better ask me before you touch one more thing!"

Out of the corner of my eye, I saw someone across the canal turn away. *I have to get away,* I thought. His anger was building way too fast. "This isn't working now," I said. "I'm getting lunch." I put down my trowel and walked toward the house. I could hear his footsteps pound the ground behind me. He squeezed my arm hard.

"Get back here! We're not finished yet."

"I'm finished for now, and I'm getting lunch. Let go of me." He was digging his fingers into my arm. I slid the screen door open with a bang and stepped into the kitchen, all the while trying to pick his fingers off my arm one by one. "*Let . . . go!*"

When I turned to face him, I could see in his eyes he wasn't with me anymore. He was in his dark place and I was in big trouble.

I struggled to break away from his hold, hoping to run into the hall bathroom. I couldn't maneuver around the butcher-block table, so I backed in between it and the sink, and I clutched a stool in front of me for protection. But I'd trapped myself.

"You don't give a shit about what's important to me, do you?" The back of his hand slammed my left cheek.

"Don't!" I screamed. "Stop it!" But he couldn't hear me anymore.

"You have no respect for me," he shouted and plucked the stool I was holding, whacking it against my arm. "Well, you better learn to." He smacked my cheek again, so hard that my head banged against the cabinet.

He threw the stool at my legs and stomped back outside. I crumpled to the floor and hugged my knees. I rested my head against the oven door. My cheek was burning. A lump on my forehead was throbbing. I closed my eyes and saw only black.

I stayed there until Isabelle meowed over to sit with me. Minutes passed, but slowly I unwound myself, stood up on shaky legs, and opened the freezer and smoothed an ice cube along my face.

I didn't cry though. Tears were nowhere near. I felt no sadness, no anger. Fear trumped them both.

27.

Like a turtle, I retracted into a small life that I could manage, and that summer the house was my shell. Jack's family became the major source of our social life.

I didn't know whether his family guessed that he hit me. I'm sure he didn't confess it, and I never said a word. If his mother had been a different kind of person, not someone who'd been abused herself and was emotionally unsteady, I might have talked to her. I wasn't sure if Jack's dad still hit her, but it was obvious to me that she was always jittery in his presence. His sisters and brothers maybe saw bruises on me like the ones they'd seen on their mother, but his anger toward me didn't build up when they were around, and they never witnessed an incident. Anyway, having grown up with violence, if they had noticed marks on me, they probably would have denied the source.

His mother often brought over the three youngest kids that summer. She liked hanging out with us and I liked entertaining the kids. Our place was like a camp. We floated on inner tubes on the canal, bounced over the waves on the bay, played cards out back, and cuddled up at night in front of TV with popcorn. Diane always had a drama going with the boy of the week. Timmy was thrilled to do anything his big brother wanted to do. Julie and I drew together with the crayons I kept on hand. I was comfortable when they were around—they liked me and I liked the person I was with them.

Things didn't lighten up with Jack's father though. I watched the way Jack interacted with him and followed his lead. Jack treated him as a man with whom he'd shared an ugly past but who'd been taught a lesson, someone who was to be included in things but kept at a distance. I was polite to his father and he to me, but we both tried to get away with saying as little as possible to each other.

Typically, when I saw him carrying his fishing equipment along the side of our backyard to his boat, I looked up and said, "Oh, hi." He looked straight ahead and said, "How ya doin'?" while walking too far away to hear an answer. He loaded things on the boat and fussed around in the cabin. When the engine started up, I called out, "Good luck!" He nodded and raised his hand as he pulled away from the dock. We never used each other's names.

Jack's dad knew he was an incredibly lucky man that his son and his wife had allowed him into their lives. Jack showed pride when his father walked across our backyard to his old wooden boat along our dock. He knew that offering his father a home for his boat was an act of forgiveness. His dad's acceptance and respectful use of the privilege was his version, I suppose, of an apology to Jack. I used these conclusions as a reason to hope that Jack could move beyond his own experience of abuse when he himself became a father.

The summer moved along smoothly now that Jack was preoccupied with finding new fishing grounds. He brought home snappers and bluefish that I baked and broiled and put into stews. The garden was growing dramatically. Jack's mother gave us her old deep fryer, so I battered and deep-fried everything I could think of—shrimp, fish, and zucchini. I even served deep-fried zucchini flowers (per Rodale) to impress whoever dined with us that summer. With Jack's big appetite I even started to make my own French fries. Like a farmer's wife, I went to bed exhausted, but never too exhausted to go along with a quickie.

I saw a lot of Lynn that summer. She had married a fellow teacher, and they lived just ten minutes away. Gary was an active, easy-going guy who accepted Jack as he was and even got Jack laughing at some of his more outrageous opinions. Gary once asked Jack to climb over the locked, chain-link fence of a furniture repair shop with him to retrieve Gary's chairs from the store that had secretly gone out of business. Jack agreed but then worried like a grandma. His resistance to the idea showed me a refreshingly cautious, law-abiding side that made our celebratory toast at their house later that night more fun. I was relieved that our husbands' relationship created a comfortable version of Jack so that I could enjoy my best friend. The four of us went out to our favorite steak house that August to celebrate our second anniversary.

I didn't have the heart-to-heart talks I used to have with Lynn though. I couldn't bring myself to tell her what my life could be like sometimes. Behind closed doors, I would sugarcoat what I said to her—"He's really a character," "He can be exhausting"—but I spared her the details of his behavior and spared myself what felt like a shameful admission. I did tell her once, "Sometimes his temper really flares up."

Often, when I thought about my life, I could convince myself that Jack and I had a reasonably normal marriage. I'd remind myself that we were furnishing and fixing up our house together just like everyone else. We went to big home improvement stores on Saturdays and talk about the pros and cons of cheap synthetic stick-on floor tiles versus the classier-looking ceramic tiles that were on sale. We filled up a giant cart at Pergament in less than an hour and then, for the entire ride home, we re-hashed our wise decisions.

Early that fall, renovating our bare attic became Jack's new project. Although it was a stuffy space we could barely stand up in, we envisioned it as a luxurious master bedroom. Once he put in electrical wiring and insulation, he spent long weekend hours up there.

One day when I was painting a bookcase in the kitchen, I heard a shout from above.

"Come up here quick."

Cupping my hand under the drippy brush, I leaned into the living room and shouted toward the stairs. "What's up?"

"I said come here. Now."

"I have a wet paint brush in my hand. I'm almost finished painting the shelves. Can't it wait?"

"Get the hell up here. Now."

"Don't talk to me like that," I yelled up from the safety of another floor, but I set the brush on the can and mounted the stairs anyway. It was almost as if my legs automatically followed his orders, since my brain was no longer working on my behalf. As I neared the top, I could see he was struggling with a huge piece of wallboard. I scrambled up to grab its corner.

"God, this is heavy!"

"You have to hold it up while I nail it on," he said breathlessly.

"There's no way I can hold this huge thing up," I said, as I strained to raise it against the sloping wall above my head.

"You got to. I can't do everything myself," he sniped, as if it had been my idea that he re-do the upstairs by himself. "Set it down a minute if you're such a pussy."

I ignored his schoolyard delivery because I could see he really needed help. "Slide the stepladder over here," I said. "I'll have to use my head and shoulder to hold it up while you nail."

That became my job for the next two weekends—holding up the thick wallboards with my head and quivering arms while he bellowed and cursed at me out of frustration. Jack had told me how furious his father used to get at him when he was a kid and dragged in to help on some project way beyond his ability. Even as a small boy, he was put in impossible situations and made to pay for it when he couldn't perform. Whenever the ghost of that young boy was in the room with us, I would give him a pass.

When the walls were painted and the carpet was laid, we moved our bedroom up there. It was basic but livable, though it annoyed me nightly to go down and up the steep stairs to use our only bathroom. *Playboy* magazines formed piles next to his side of the bed. The lava lamp shone from the floor in a corner. Below the window a spider plant with its jagged, far-reaching offshoots demanded water.

I was proud of what a big construction job Jack had accomplished up there, but mounting those stairs to go to bed at night, and taking in those sloping walls as I neared the top, often gave me a smack of claustrophobia.

28.

In November of '72 my tenth high school reunion came up. I rarely went back to the Philadelphia area and had lost touch with all but one good friend. I wanted to see my old friends and find out what they were doing, and mostly, to see what their marriages looked like. But I was torn between going, which I desperately wanted to do, and staying away, which is what my instinct told me to do. Taking Jack to an event where he was out of his comfort zone would be a huge risk. Being away from Jack for a weekend was out of the question. I'd have a barrage of negativity to face before and after the trip.

I'm over-thinking this, I decided, a few weeks before the event. I'd like to have Jack come to my reunion, and if I told him that, maybe it would set the right tone. To give it my best shot, I caught him in his plant room when he was working on the freshwater aquarium.

"I just called Paula about our tenth reunion. She wants us to stay with them so we can all go together."

He peered into the tank and moved a stick gently along the bottom. "What? Oh yeah. Your reunion. Don't I have a wrestling meet that weekend?"

"Nope. You're free." I moved right next to him and watched as he pushed the gravel around a new plant. "I really hope you'll come with me."

"Okay."

"Really?"

"Sure," he said. I glided out of the room beaming as if I had discovered a new superpower.

Jack and I drove to Philadelphia the Saturday afternoon of the reunion and settled into Paula and Kevin's house, near the country club where the reunion was being held. That evening the four of us walked into the banquet room together. My hands were sweaty as I picked through the nametags on the table and surveyed the crowd.

"You gotta show me which one is Doug," Jack whispered from behind.

He was thinking about my old boyfriend? "Why? Are you going to punch him out?" I said, before realizing how unwise it was to joke around when he was uptight.

"Ha, ha," he sneered. "I want to see what kind of jerk you dated in high school."

"I don't see him, Jack. Maybe he's not coming." I wouldn't have dared to mention how disappointed I would have been if that were true. "Let's get something to drink," I said instead.

During the cocktail hour, Jack stayed close to my side except when he headed to the bar for another drink. *Good,* I thought, *maybe it'll help him loosen up.*

I squealed when I saw old girlfriends, and I introduced Jack all around. "He's so cute," a few whispered to me, as if we were huddled in front of our lockers. I chatted and laughed and oohed and aahed at baby pictures while Jack downed rye and gingers. The only time I gave Jack much thought—I was drinking a lot too—was when I talked to Doug, whom I'd casually pointed out earlier. I made sure to move away from him after a few minutes of chatting, since I figured wherever Jack was he would be watching.

We sat with four other couples at the dinner. The women were my closest girlfriends, so we talked without a break. The husbands, all strangers to each other, were quiet and focused on their food and drinks. As the dinner wound down, Paula and I left the table and circulated, looking for people we'd missed. We all had weathered the storms of adolescence together from seventh through twelfth grade in our public junior/senior high school. Everyone had so much to report—new jobs, promotions, marriages, kids. In those years, by the age of twenty-eight, almost everyone was married.

After dinner a DJ set up and oldies blasted out of the speakers. A couple of booming strains of the Kingsmen singing "Louie, Louie" and I came alive. Jack didn't dance, as he'd announced, and I loved to, so I partnered up with whomever (usually another girl or two) or no one at all now that we weren't jitterbugging anymore. It was exhilarating. I was sixteen again.

I knew that was not going to sit well with Jack, but I didn't care. *My high school reunion, for God's sake,* I reasoned. *It's* my *big night!*

On the way back to the house Jack and I sat in the backseat of Kevin's car. Jack leaned his back against his door to face me. In a stage whisper, he snapped, "I shouldn't have to go pull my wife off the fucking dance floor."

"You're right. You shouldn't," I felt like yelling, but instead I murmured, "You should let her have fun with her old buddies."

"And expect me to sit alone waiting for hours!" he said. Paula squirmed in the front seat.

"For hours? Come off it." The good vibes from the party were empowering me. "You weren't alone. Kevin and other people were with you, and you knew I was dying to dance."

"That is so goddamn *typical* of you, acting like some prom slut and . . ." He kept the accusations coming, in the backseat of the car, walking into the house, in the wall-papered guest room separated by only a thin wall from the master bedroom and down the hall from where their two little girls were sleeping.

On and on it went, into the wee hours . . . "You better not turn your back on me!"

I could barely face Paula in the morning. She was now a witness to how worked-up and angry Jack got. How I kowtowed to him. How I said anything, did anything to make him shut up, because, when the yelling stopped, she might have even heard us having sex.

Back at home after the night when shame put its enduring stain on my friendship with Paula, I did what I had been teaching myself to do—I went through the motions of living as unremarkably as possible, and I waited. Waited until things got better. They always did. I knew they would get bad again, but I also knew they would get better again. That was the jerky, unpredictable pattern I accepted as my life. After an *incident* Jack might say, "I'm sorry," or hug me without a word. Most often he simply moved more slowly around me and forced himself to look directly at me when he had something to say. I took it all as an apology and went on with life the way it was.

29.

Only at my job did I feel truly alive. There I didn't talk to people about "us." (That's how I thought of my home life—"us" being the couple who had made a pact to accept his rages with her vow of silence.) Because I was an animated, good-natured person at school, I'm sure some people assumed I was a happily single woman, sitting at her desk after school hours to do paperwork and make calls. No pictures of a husband or kids on her desk. Showing up by herself at TGIFs.

I studied the marriages I saw at school. How do people do it? Dean, a quiet young counselor, went home promptly after school and never mentioned his wife's name. *She must wear the pants in that family,* I figured.

The wife of a flirtatious young counselor, Mark, showed up promptly whenever the faculty got together after hours. *She must need to watch him like a hawk.*

The wife of Lou, a fifty-something high-strung Italian, seemed to float imperceptibly above his office. "Norma told me that . . .", "Norma and I ate there . . .", "Norma just called and said . . ." *That clinging would suffocate me!*

The marriage I studied the most belonged to Grace. She and her husband, both fair-haired and freckled, played golf together regularly on weekends and enjoyed the evening ritual of chatting over a cocktail. They delighted in their six kids, who looked like their clones. *Ah, they make it all look so easy!*

The counselor I got to know best was Maxine, a handsome

brunette in her late-forties with great bone-structure and a nose job. She and her husband Sid, a combative leader in the county teachers' union, had both been married once before. When she spoke of Sid, it was clear that their relatively new marriage had a lot of passion in it. *Even at their age!* I marveled.

Studying others was a futile exercise; there was little for me to learn by watching these couples. I took away only one lesson: their marriages are all normal and mine is not. The less people know about us, the better.

At home that winter I threw myself into fix-up projects while Jack was busy with coaching. The house continued to be a blank canvas for me. I had never realized how satisfying it was to refurbish things. I hadn't seen a woman do that before—and certainly not on TV. Harriet Nelson and Donna Reed were too dressed up in their pearls and heels. Applying smelly chemicals to furniture, scraping paint off, hammering nails? I did it all because it was important to me. I saw it as getting the house ready for a family.

All the major renovation jobs were done. Jack was finishing up his Master's program. We each had a growing savings account. Life was moving faster than I could imagine. My twenties would be over in two years. A day didn't go by without me saying something to myself like, "We could fit a crib right along this wall," or "There's room under this window for a toy chest." So three years after living with Jack and seven years after starting the powerful birth control pills they prescribed in the '60s, I told Jack I wanted to stop taking them.

I felt I could tell what he would be like with children by the way he was lighthearted and loving with his younger brothers and sisters, and, of course, the cats. I had never known anyone who loved and cared for his pets like Jack did. He would be an active, involved father, I was sure, although I didn't really know how to visualize one. I had told Jack how my own father had parented in absentia, not away from the premises but absent all the same. Jack was attentive when I talked about my family, so I told him things I had never talked about before. My voice was shaky when I told him how my father was in no way involved in our daily lives. I didn't remember him ever asking me one question. Never, "What did you do today?" "Where are you going?" or "Did you have fun?" Nothing that would ever show that he saw me as an individual rather than part of the entity known as "the girls."

That also meant he never yelled at me or hit me. The only times he was in charge of us when we were youngsters was on Friday nights when my mother went to church choir practice. Doris and I would cook up all sorts of shady things to do. At some point, most likely when he was afraid my mother would come home and see that we were still up at 9:45, he would tighten his face and assume a scary position—an easy task for a tall man facing two little girls—and say "I'm going to take off my belt now . . . " We knew the fun was over so we'd squeal and run to our beds giggling all the way. Yet for the remainder of the week, it felt as though he weren't there, as if that Friday night he had been a babysitter who went back to his own place.

30.

After years of trying to avoid pregnancy, I was shocked when month after month my period made its remarkably punctual appearance. It never occurred to me that I might have trouble getting pregnant. A college friend had teased me about having childbearing hips. A gynecologist (male) had once told me I was lucky to have such painful periods because it meant things were working well.

My sister had had no trouble. I thought more and more about the year before, when she had been expecting her second baby around Christmas. Her doctor, not wanting to be on call over the holidays, said the baby was large enough to deliver early, so he scheduled the date of birth for December 16 when he would induce it.

When the 16th came, I waited for the long-distance call from my mother all day. When I hadn't heard from her by bedtime that night, I assumed something had come up for the doctor, and he had rescheduled. On the afternoon of the next day, I checked in with my mother at home.

"What's going on? When's Doris going to have the baby?"

"Oh, my goodness, you don't know? She had *twins* yesterday. After the first one was born, the doctor realized there was a second smaller one behind the first! Two healthy little girls. We're all so excited."

Wow! That's unbelievable, I thought, *but . . . she forgot to call me?* I sat with the pain of being left out, but I felt only mild surprise. Since childhood I had learned to be the one to handle things on my own, because my mother was busy dealing with my high-maintenance sister.

But here it is, a year later, I thought, *and I'm ready to get pregnant. My sister's three little girls will be first cousins to the kids I'll have.* I felt the vise of jealousy tighten as I pictured my dear little nieces but shook it off. It would happen soon for me.

During that winter the twenty-seventh day of my reliably regular biological month was like Christmas Eve. Maybe this time I would be surprised! But the unwelcome present I got at some point the next day was a bloody spot on my pants and strong cramps. I got the sinking feeling that we were going to be one of the ten percent of couples the books talked about—those unable to conceive within twelve months. Each month when my period came, I felt a stab of sadness with a pinch of shame mixed in. I was glad we hadn't spread the word that we were trying. It was hard enough for me to tell Jack it had come once again. "That's okay," he said. "Give it time," and he pulled me to his chest for a hug.

I pored over the infertility section of every book I could get my hands on at a bookstore or the library. I read and re-read that section of *Our Bodies, Ourselves.* Most books said it often took months of trying, so no need to consult a doctor until a year was up. My head and my heart were ready, but my body wasn't there yet, I guessed. I didn't question whether it had anything to do with the stress I lived with. How could I tell anyway? From then on, I separated my desire for a child from any concern about the condition of our marriage. It's hard for me to understand now how I could possibly do that, but I did.

When it had been a year since I stopped taking the Pill, I met with the OB/GYN I was assigned to at Jack's healthcare plan's clinic. This mid-island facility was an unwelcoming, crowded place with harried doctors and officious staffers. Sitting behind his desk, the gynecologist made no eye contact with me as I answered the questions he read from a list. Was he even listening? The only time he looked up at me was when I answered that we had sex every night. After the questioning, he mechanically listed the usual testing protocol, and then he told me to take off everything and put on the paper robe for my internal exam.

As the doctor felt my lymph glands and neck he slid the paper robe down and completely off me (with no nurse present).

"Can't I have that or some sheet over me?"

"No, no. Lie back down. I won't be long." He pushed my shoulder and roughly performed the internal exam. As he probed, he mentioned that my uterus was tipped, but said it was fairly common and most likely wasn't the cause.

Everything about that experience reinforced my irrational, but naggingly present, sense that I was guilty of something and being punished for it. Since his exam found nothing definitive, I left the office worrying about what might lie ahead for me.

After hearing about my tipped uterus, I read an article where the author recommended putting pillows under the buttocks right after sex on the key days, so I kept an extra one next to my side of the bed. After two fruitless months of trying that, we made an appointment to have Jack's sperm tested. No answers there. "His numbers and motility are excellent!" the doctor reported.

During my last exam at this clinic, where a dye was inserted into my uterus through the cervix to allow pictures of the uterus and tubes, I gasped loudly from the pain. The nurse who held my hand warned my gynecologist I was losing color. "Keep her still," he yelled. "I'm not finished."

At home, within an hour of the procedure my ears started itching, followed by my eyes, my rectum, and then my throat. As my breathing got shallow, Jack rushed me to the emergency room where they immediately inserted an IV drip. "Oh, yes," the doctor later said as if it had been too insignificant to mention, "Some women do get a serious allergic reaction to the dye."

After the testing showed no results, conversations about pregnancy stopped between Jack and me. I was furious at the way the doctor had treated me and devastated about not being able to get pregnant. I buried that burning hot coal, fueled equally by sadness and anger, deep inside me, and without letting on I wasn't the woman I thought I was, I went about my life.

31.

I remember that winter of '73 – '74, not for the gasoline crisis with its skyrocketing prices, endless lines at the pumps, and fights over rationed gas. I remember it as the time I fell in love with a man I worked with.

Ted was hired as a counselor at Heritage the year before. He was a substantial guy with curly dark hair and a keen sense of humor. During his first year there I might have described him as a "straight arrow," someone I wasn't especially drawn to with his desktop pictures of a brunette wife sporting a '50's hairstyle and two dimpled little girls. He wore tortoise-shell glasses and preppy clothes at a time when lots of male teachers our age had hair tickling their shoulders and wore shirts with Nehru collars. At the time, I fit in with most other young women on staff—braless, with uneven long hair, and skirts the size of two dinner napkins.

I felt the first touch of what was to grow into a serious connection at a weekly guidance department meeting, a place more likely to produce yawns than passion. That day, Ted, who'd shown himself to be competent and ambitious about his career, sat appropriately at the right hand of our chairman. The three oldest counselors were already seated, able to get there early and relaxed since fewer students consulted them each day. We younger counselors took turns rushing in at the last minute, depending on who was currently dealing with the ever-present "emergency."

As I slipped into the room I noticed Ted look up. "Well, here she comes," he announced like Bert Parks, "Miss America." He gestured for me to sit next to him. "What's your talent today?" He bordered on corny sometimes.

"Don't worry," I said slumping into the chair and plunking an armload of papers in front of me. "When everyone gets here, I'll begin twirling my baton on the table."

He turned to me and smiled. A smile I hadn't seen before.

When we got to New Business on our agenda, I reported that some seniors still didn't have their list of colleges to apply to and were too busy with fall activities and work to visit schools. They didn't have enough information to decide, so I suggested they go to another high school's college fair. "I'd love to see us have our own," I added, "maybe in spring, for juniors."

"That's a terrific idea," Ted said. "We could have reps from technical and business schools too, and you know the Armed Services, they'll definitely want to come." Tapping his hand on my arm he said "I'd like to work on it with you."

The rest of the agenda wasn't groundbreaking that day. What went on at the table was. (I don't know what this says about human sexuality, but it's so real to me I can feel it to this day.) Ted's folded right arm rested on the table about an inch away from my left arm. I was aware that neither of us was moving away, and it became clear to me that it was intentional on both our parts. I could feel something transpiring, an almost-tickle of the generous dark hair on his arm and the light fuzz on my arm, as they grazed each other as if we were emitting a signal, as animals do. I might have thought I was imagining this if he hadn't stumbled while speaking to the group, shot a peripheral glance at me, then cleared his throat before continuing. After that moment we never again spoke without the sense of a shared secret.

He and I spent weeks that fall hammering out the minutiae of our program, amassing a list of schools and colleges and then dividing them up to contact. Ted was confident and comfortable dealing with problems that came up, and we usually found something comical about them. During our conversations I was tuned into how well we worked together and, though it was never spoken out loud during those weeks, we both learned the surprising lesson that mutual respect could be a turn-on.

On the last day before the two-week holiday break, the faculty held its after- school Christmas party. Ted and I stood squeezed together, talking about our new project. As we refilled our glasses, the conversation bounced around and our smiles were more telling. I threw out remarks to make him laugh and he touched my arm or back in amusement. The touches began to linger.

"Bye-bye!" and "Merry Christmas!" filled the air. People drifted out, headed for home and their families. As the bar emptied, Ted and I walked through the lobby to the front door. I reached up to hug him good-bye—this, in the days before everybody hugged everybody. As we pulled back with our faces still close, our eyes told each other what we wanted. We kissed longer and harder than was smart to do in public. I would feel that kiss, taste it, and savor it for the whole vacation.

At home during that break I was like a teenager with a secret crush that made me beam and was on my mind most of the day. I didn't let anyone know. It was none of their business.

Back in school after New Year's Day, the second semester approached, and students were in and out of the guidance suite all day. I was able to focus on their issues—exams coming up, making up missing work, changing second semester classes—as long as Ted didn't walk by my door. I was jelly then.

In the line-up of counseling offices, there were three cubicles between his and mine. We all kept our offices open unless the folding doors were closed for privacy. Ted and I both came up with reasons to stroll along the row to see if each other's doors were open, and we could stop in for quick hello. Even if he was busy, his expression would light up when he saw me at his door. For the first time in my life, I could put a face on the picture of a man I would like to be married to.

At 3:10, his office exerted its magnetic force on me. Because it was coaching season for Jack, he'd be at school for a couple extra hours. Ted didn't need to rush home either, he said. His wife and girls were out at their activities. We were content to meet there at school with no one around, until one day Ted suggested we go out for a drink.

The two of us sat at a small table in an empty bar a few towns away. As soon as our legs touched, they curled around each other's. Our eyes darted around the dark room, looking for any sign of movement near the doorway. It was obvious he also was a rank beginner at this scheming. When the bartender came over, I ordered a gin and tonic and, to this day, I can hear Ted ordering his drink—a Harvey Wallbanger.

"Well, aren't you the Lounge Lizard!" I said. "Harvey Wallbanger? What's that?"

"Poor baby, you don't get around much do you?"

"No, I'm not part of the seedy bar scene," I said as I sat there in a seedy bar.

"It's vodka, Galliano, and orange juice. Want a taste?"

He handed me his glass, and I put my lips exactly where he had put his. I took a sip. "You're being taken," I said. "It's a Screwdriver they're charging more for."

We had only the one drink then hurried out to his station wagon (of course!) and made out like horny sixteen-year-olds. That first time we met outside of school was so much more than "just a drink." It was an event that proclaimed to us, "It works! You two can have a private life together as long as no one else knows." The fact that I was married to Jack somehow seemed beside the point. But where were the brakes? I wonder now. Where were the thoughts about the other people involved or an awareness of what the consequences might be? I guess it's possible to forget about anything, even a firestorm coming your way, when you're satisfying a craving.

At one of our after-school talks in Ted's office, we decided we would get together after an evening PTA meeting. The promise of being together in the dark of night signified that we were getting deeper into what we had started. It was all I could think about for the days leading up to it.

That night Ted suggested I tail his station wagon to the place he'd picked, a secluded woodsy spot. We parked and I slipped into his car.

"Why do I suddenly feel like I'm in high school?" I said. "Except there's no giant screen to look at through the windshield."

He laughed and pulled me tight against him. "You're great," he said in his smooth bass tone, brushing my hair away from my face. "I've wanted this for so long."

"I want you, too," I said and meant it from my heart on down.

Ted released the back seats to make a bed for us then grabbed a tape to put in the player. I smiled at how much thought my straight-arrow boyfriend must have given to this moment when I heard Roberta Flack purr " . . . The first time ever I lay with you and felt your heart . . ." He reached into his pocket and pulled out a condom. I nodded. Then with little room to move and lots of clothing between us, we threw ourselves into sex.

32.

From that night on, I ached for his smile, his hands, his voice, his smell. But the logistics of meeting outside of school were thorny for both of us. Mostly we found ways to sit close together after school in some out-of-the-way spot to drink, talk, and laugh. We met in motels five times after our woodsy night. Our sex wasn't the bodice-ripping kind. More like married-for-a-year kind—exciting enough but slower and more comfortable. We whispered to each other throughout. As the months went by we both started using the word "love."

"If only we were in Cincinnati," we would joke. It was our short-hand for "Everything would be perfect if only our other lives didn't exist." The trouble was, I wanted my other life to disappear much, much more than Ted wanted his to.

One day I told Ted, "I want to leave Jack." It came out of my mouth as if I'd been rehearsing for days, though I cringed having it hang in the air between us. It showed a certainty that frightened me: I want you to be my husband and I assume you want me to be your wife.

Leaving his wife and family would be hard, he said. He wanted to be with me so he'd find a way, he said. He'd have to think about how to talk to her about splitting up, he said. She'd lost her father as a child so it was especially hard for him to break it to her, he said. Then, yes, he said three weeks later, he knew he'd promised he'd get it out in the open that weekend, but it had been a special family time. Every word stung.

After the next weekend, when he'd promised he would absolutely, positively have the conversation with his wife, he confessed, "The words just won't come out of my mouth."

Of course the words wouldn't come out of his mouth. He was a good man who loved his family. I knew that about him, and as crazy as it sounds, I loved him for it. I pretended that part of his life, those other people, didn't exist, just as I pretended Jack didn't exist. I was living in an altered state of reality, as though I had found a simple way to change lives. As if, when I told Jack about Ted, I would say only "good-bye" and move into that new life.

I don't remember driving home. The whole world had turned a fuzzy gray. I wanted to get home fast and let out the misery building inside me. When I walked into the house, Jack sprinted toward the door from the kitchen. He shouldn't have been home yet. I stifled a groan.

"Why are you late?" he said.

I wasn't ready for him and his questions. Without hearing what I was saying, I uttered, "I was meeting with someone about something." I couldn't look at him.

"What the hell does that mean? You were *meeting with someone*?? You weren't *at a meeting*. You were *meeting with someone*. Who was that *someone* that kept you late?"

"Ah, Jack, it's school stuff. What does it matter? I'm late. I'm sorry."

"I'll tell you why it matters. I don't like that fucking look on your face. You're hiding something. Who were you with?" I flinched, expecting him to come toward me. But he didn't. He backed up, as if preparing for a blow. He looked ten years old to me then, not a batterer but the victim.

"I've been having an affair but it's over."

I was shocked to hear myself tell him. Maybe I thought Jack would throw me out of the house, and he would be the one to decide our marriage was over. It strikes me now that I was deliberately tossing a bomb into our home, certain that he and I would not survive the devastation.

Instead, Jack demanded details. The grilling was relentless. Is it Tom? Ed? Bill? Joel? Howie? He guessed every good-looking guy we knew. Inside the first hour of questioning I caved in. I knew his questions would never end.

"It's Ted," I said. The name was almost indiscernible from my sigh.

"Ted??" he said as if he didn't know who that was even though they'd met a few times. Then he repeated, "Ted?" and I realized he couldn't grasp that it was Ted I'd been with. Not some handsome lothario. Just Ted.

Then the cross examination really began. Jack wanted more than the human brain is equipped to recall. He pumped me for information as if the details gave him power. How long? How often? Where? When? What was said? Who did what to whom? Hour after hour of questioning. Oral? Anal? Orgasms?

How could I not have seen this coming?

As soon as school ended on the day after my confession, I slipped into Ted's office and told him Jack knew. I didn't know that it would be our final conversation.

That night at home Jack announced, "I decided I'm going to meet with Ted."

"Go ahead." What else could I say? He'd hardly asked me for permission. Jack called him at school the next day, and after work he drove to wherever they were meeting. I suffered at home, sitting in a tight ball on the living room couch, rocking back and forth, waiting for it to be over and eager to find out what had happened. Mainly, did Ted make it out alive?

When Jack came home, I could tell from his account of the hour they'd sat in a restaurant that Ted had allowed Jack the role of the "wronged one," a role Jack was comfortable in. He didn't need to lash out. Ted's apology to Jack must have been heartfelt, because Jack accepted it. Their understanding was that Ted and I were finished.

When I saw Ted's face the next day at school, I knew I had lost not only the person I loved but also my friend. His look exposed what I felt—an ugly mix of shame and fear and regret—something that did not go away for either of us for the rest of the year. We never again smiled at each other. Late that spring, he announced at a department meeting that he had gotten an administrative job elsewhere.

Every ounce of hope I had that I could live a different life with a different man vanished. I didn't have any time to wallow in sadness though, for I was anointed The Guilty One. During the next months Jack asked questions about Ted and me when he was bothered, but over time the questions stopped. Jack told his family about my affair and the emotional pain of what he was going through, "Just for support," he said. It gave him a power that he relished, and those next few months brought one of the calmest periods of our marriage. I couldn't help but feel a flood of relief from the gentleness he showed me. I didn't understand then how his behavior was working to tighten our bond.

If I had owned a diary in the months that followed my affair, though I wouldn't have dared put my thoughts down on paper, I might have written, "I feel stuck here. As if I'm stuck to Jack forever, with an invisible but super-powerful glue." Crazy glue.

33.

Do I remember this or is it rather something I'm imagining as I think about the young woman I was then, during those months after Ted?

I see my younger self in our tiny living room, standing straight and still, staring out the picture window onto the street, not looking at anything. I am wide-eyed with no emotion showing on my face. Hope is almost visibly bleeding out of my body, the hope that I might someday live with a gentle man who is my friend as much as my lover.

What is going on inside that young woman, with the long brown hair and the tired eyes? I would say that she has suffered a loss that is too big to name. She is discovering that all along she has wanted a man who would allow her the safety and the space to grow into herself.

She feels so alone and she wishes that weren't true. But she's practiced at relying on herself for comfort and support. She has work that brings out the best in her. She has found a creative impulse in her hands; it doesn't yet come from her heart, but it will. She must try to build what she can with the life she has chosen, but it often feels heavy enough to crush her into nothingness.

The "real life" she expected to have is on hold or never to be. She is simply going through the motions. Driving to work, listening to her students—her kids, she calls them—helping them as best she can, taking care of her husband, her home, and her cats, watching her period come and go each month, and always, crossing her fingers that it will be a calm night.

She's treading water, understanding that there's no vessel coming to rescue her.

34.

For the next months Jack and I didn't say a word about trying to get pregnant. No thermometers, pencils, or charts by the bed but lots of sex with no protection. I wonder now was it guilt or shame or maybe anger that allowed me to ignore the possibility of getting pregnant and bringing a baby into our life, slight as I thought the chance. Whatever it was, telltale tampons sat bundled in the trash each month.

Being creative, using my hands, and staying busy brought me the closest thing to joy that was missing at home and now even at school. I took my camera with me everywhere I went. I collected scraps of fabric and started on a quilt. I painted our bathroom a glossy purple. I made drapes for the bedroom. Yet, while I tried to fix the house up, Jack tried to fill it.

Every room felt like his personal locker. Catalogues for gardening and stereos and boat equipment were all over the house. Fishing lures were sprinkled around the kitchen counter. New fish tank tubing curled next to the front door. Upstairs, on the carpet under the only bedroom window, sat two moist trays of sunflower seedlings.

"Geez, Jack, I can't get close enough to this stuck window to open it up," I told him. "Can't you put these trays someplace else?"

"No. Don't you touch them," he bellowed. "They'll only survive in a southern exposure. Leave them right where they are."

"Well, maybe I'll only survive if I can get the damn window open for some fresh air."

"Ex-cuuuse me, your Highness. I didn't realize you were more important than everything else."

I stomped toward the door, bumping into a watering can, around a pile of ungraded tests, and vaulted over muddy jeans to get out of there. I rushed down the stairs and into the small room next to Jack's plant room (our second bedroom according to the realtor). Looking around I could feel it turning into something else. I would claim it. I would make a place for myself in that house.

Over the next months I dove into decorating my room, furnishing it with second-hand things I'd found or with things I made. I brought all my books from around the house and, in the fashion of the day, made a long bookshelf from two wood planks and eight bricks. On the top shelf I put a philodendron on a macramé placemat and a Mateus bottle with clumps of dripped wax. Before long I picked up a cheap couch at a garage sale—Scandinavian style I called it, but it was basically a plain old-fashioned couch, so stark that I bought a loud geometric print fabric and re-covered it myself. The room now sounds to me like a museum diorama.

I had just started taking an adult education oil painting class at the nearby high school, and I set up my easel in my new room. I filled the closet with my painting supplies and canvases. Before long I hung two of my paintings on the wall. They were landscapes I'd copied from calendar photos—creativity was not valued in those night classes—but I loved looking at my respectable versions of the idyllic scenes.

I hadn't behaved like a creative person or an artist since I was a little girl. In kindergarten I had created a play about turtles that my class put on in front of the entire school. (I still remember the joy of having a second-grader tell me afterwards in the girls' room that it was "very good.") A box of twenty-four Crayola crayons was my favorite toy. Throughout my childhood I had entertained myself by drawing and sometimes Scotch-taping my drawings together so they could be scrolled and unrolled like a film for any audience I could find. My mother must have said something like "That's nice, dear." But she never referred to any of this. Being unique, having a talent, or standing out were frowned-upon qualities. In my home, "Showing Off" was one of the seven deadly sins.

My creativity had been in hiding during my teens and early twenties as if once I turned thirteen I had forgotten who I'd been for the last twelve years. School didn't help. Girls in Honors classes took another foreign language as an elective, not art. But during my junior year of high school, the counselor gave our class the Kuder Occupational Interest Survey, and I've held onto the 3x5 card with my results of that test ever since. It read like the nine most exciting jobs anyone could have: *Author, Actress, Artist, Architect, Cartoonist, Curator, Editor, Photographer,* and *Vocational Counselor.* There was no *Teacher* on the list; that surprised me. The two strongest adults in my life, my mother and my Aunt Helen were teachers, and Doris who was away at college that year was headed in that direction too. No one in my extended family did any of the things on my list or had one as a hobby. I couldn't understand how the counselor had come up with it. That exotic grouping of jobs felt like something pulled from an Ouija board, and I knew at sixteen that I was lucky to have that cool list to show to my friends, future *Librarians, Accountants, Secretaries,* and *Bookkeepers.* What I rediscovered at twenty-nine was that test had nailed it, and I was a happier person when I was creating.

My room became the place where I regularly meditated before and after school, since it was easier to quiet my mind and repeat my mantra when Jack wasn't around. But even though I referred to it as "my room," it wasn't exclusively mine. I had to share it with Jack in the evening since that's where we had our 13" television. Like most married couples, we had "our shows," the ones we'd stop what we were doing to flop down on the couch. We'd catch *Rowan and*

Martin's Laugh In on Mondays. (You *had* to watch it to understand the origin of the kooky lines people threw out during the following week.) Then on Tuesday nights, we were there for *Hawaii 5-0*, one of Jack's favorites. The show we tried never to miss was *All in the Family*. The hippie son-in-law versus the pig-headed conservative father struck a chord with Jack. For me, that family was as foreign but as funny as you could get.

I didn't mind sharing. No angry words were ever spoken in that space during a TV show or for at least half an hour after it was over.

35.

One evening that spring when Jack came in, I was leaning over the dishwasher as if each item I loaded weighed twenty pounds. It was only 8:30, but the school day had been draining, and I couldn't wait to finish up, climb into bed, and read. Jack slid along the counter behind me and pressed against me, his arms around my hips and hands rubbing my belly. Slowly they moved down and stroked between my legs. I gritted my teeth. His hands felt intrusive, foreign, and I had to stifle an urge to scream, "Get your hands off me."

Instead I forced myself to chirp, "Oh, lover boy, not tonight, okay? I'm pooped."

"You can't be too 'pooped' for me, can you?" He brushed the hair off the back of my neck and kissed it. His lips sent a chill down my back.

"I had a crazy day, and I'm so tired I can't see straight," I said, trying to sound light. "Tonight, my dearie, I can resist even you." He pulled back sharply. My radar must have been off. I hadn't picked up on the intensity of his need, but it was one of those nights when I simply did not have the option. I was not entitled to say "No" at 8:00, or 10:00, or even midnight.

"You always want whatever you want," he spit out, "and never think of what I want."

By then I had stopped asking, "How can you mean that?" because that question was never answered. At some point, just seconds before, what he was saying became The Truth. Now, questioning The Truth, I became an even bigger Shit. He was going to say it again and again. And if I didn't go along, I had to be punished.

"Come on, Jack. I'm exhausted. I need to relax and get some sleep," I said, "Let's hug, okay?"

He leaned back as if I were radioactive. "Get off me!" His eyes widened as though he'd just discovered another Horrible Truth. "It's all about *you* and never *me*."

I froze in place. I knew that look on his face. He was frantically creating a story to hide behind. That accusation, that fireball he spewed out into the air, was his armor. And from inside the armor, he didn't give a damn what the enemy felt, and by that time I had become simply The Enemy, and The Enemy must be hurt.

He backhanded my cheekbone and nose with his knuckles. It felt like a knife slicing my face but then came sudden, flaming heat. He bounded out of the room and up the stairs. I only heard, ". . . selfish bitch."

I curled in on myself, my clammy hands covering my face. I dropped them only when I could bear looking around me, at my kitchen, my house, my life. The world I lived in with this man.

I shuffled into the bathroom and looked at myself in the mirror, staring as if I were a stranger. *Her nose might be broken. There's blood seeping onto her lip. She needs help.*

I grabbed a handful of tissues and stepped back into the kitchen, gathering my purse and keys from the table. I snuck out to my car at the curb and slipped in. Maybe Jack could hear the car start, but I no longer cared. Even if he did, he wouldn't have enough time to get to his car and follow me. With one eye half shut and one hand pressing a tissue to my nose, I drove to the emergency entrance of our nearby hospital.

The woman at the desk looked directly at me but showed no alarm. *Maybe I shouldn't be here,* I thought. *Maybe this is no big deal in an emergency room.* But I took the forms she gave me, filled them out, and took a seat. I picked up a magazine and stared at a page, but I jumped when I heard a woman in white call my name—*my name doesn't belong here.* She took me to a bright, chilly room and helped me onto the table. She came back with a warmed blanket to wrap around me. I thanked her as if she'd thrown me a lifesaver in the sea.

I waited for hours it seemed, though it was probably fifteen minutes, until a doctor and nurse come into the room. The doctor stood at my knees and inspected the skin around my cheek and nose. In a quiet voice he asked, "How did this happen?"

"My husband got angry and punched me," I said. I was about to go on, but I caught myself. Suddenly it was clear to me—that was the beginning and the end of it. What happened before or after didn't matter. He does this. As the nurse helped me lie down, she looked at the doctor, scrunched her lips, and shook her head. I took that to mean I was not the first woman with such an answer that night.

The nurse wiped my cheek with a cold antiseptic that stung where Jack's wedding ring must have scraped. She bandaged it. I gasped when the doctor touched my nose. "Nothing's broken, fortunately," he said as the nurse carefully slid cotton into my nostril. "There's a little bleeding now. Lie here and rest with this cold pack."

As I lay back, I waited for something else, anything else he could do or say to help me, but he only looked at me. I could feel him wishing he could help more too, but all he knew to say that night was, "In a half hour, you can go back home."

36.

Jack didn't look straight at me the next day. He spoke to me more quietly, even asking if he could get something for me from the drugstore. Things had shifted slightly in our home. I had left. I had told someone what he had done. I had *shown* someone what he had done.

I was quiet that day. I had learned early on that saying nothing after an incident was the fastest way to peace in the house. I didn't want to risk throwing it out to him and starting that ugly, unknowable thing up again. I usually made the naïve assumption I was helping him too—letting him stew about what he had done and maybe feel bad for a while. But on the day after my Emergency Room visit I wanted to have my voice heard.

Jack was in the plant room watering. I stood in the doorway, leaning against the jam. My bruised face was lit from the window. "You've got to do something, Jack."

He turned toward me with a puzzled look, then saw my face and looked away.

"You have to find a way to stop doing this," I said.

"I know," he said. "I know." His jaw quivered as he fought against breaking down. "I saw it at home. I don't want to hurt you. I love you so much."

"I know you do. I love you too," I told him, "but this can't keep happening." In spite of it all, I still called my feelings "love." I deeply felt the connection we had, that thing we called love. It was powerful. Part animal attraction, part neediness, part yearning, part hope. But it was not exactly love.

As I looked at him that day I saw a sadness seeping from him and encircling him like an aura. I felt sorry for him, but I wished I didn't. He had terrified me. He had hurt me. Yet in leaving the house the night before, I saw that I was beginning to find the courage to take care of myself.

Sitting at the kitchen counter one night a week later, staring into the closed-in porch we'd renovated early on, I thought about our enthusiasm and pride at fixing up the house. We had driven to big antique markets in rural Pennsylvania to buy furnishings and decorations. We'd had such a good time together, watching each other gush over different vendors' goods, that we went back again and again, first for a Franklin stove, then later for oak clocks and dressers. On those antique-hunting excursions to the Pennsylvania Dutch country, away from the pressures and provocations of everyday life, Jack let down his guard and relaxed. We drove around the countryside and ate potpie at restaurants with community tables. And we laughed.

I decided we should take a road trip for our spring break coming up the following month. Florida was the obvious pick for me. Every summer of my childhood, my family drove in our old Dodge down to Miami to visit my father's parents. My fondest childhood memories take place in that car headed south, my father driving with his window open and left arm folded out. The hot air streamed in on me, sitting atop a slippery hound's-tooth suitcase that didn't fit in the trunk. Those trips must have also been memorable for me as the rare times we felt like a four-person family.

I wanted to show Jack the sunbaked state I loved and the highlights along the way—the Skyline Drive through Virginia, the South of the Border shop at the North/South Carolina line, and Route 301 through small-town Georgia, the glass bottom boats of Silver Springs and the acrobatic water skiers of Cypress Gardens. I hoped he would love it, too.

Jack dove into the planning. He fashioned a makeshift RV out of his new VW bus for camping on the way down, by replacing the back seats with a large piece of plywood for a bed. My contribution was a set of curtains that attached to the windows with large suction cups.

The stay in Ft. Lauderdale allowed us to feel like we were on a real vacation. We played tennis on public courts, bodysurfed in the ocean, and played highly competitive rounds of miniature golf. On the last night of our stay, the man at the desk of the motel told us about a great deal—a free dinner and drinks at a new hotel close to the beach. All we'd have to do is listen to a presentation about an inland community under development.

We felt like real buddies then, sitting at dinner, watching a woman set up a map of the new development. Jack and I shared conspiratorial looks over our glasses of wine. On the display boards, most of the half-acre plots were red (sold), a few were yellow (under contract) and not many were green (available). Along the large lake only three lots were still available. During dessert, a man with an unnatural tan and a well-fitting suit spoke enthusiastically. At two different times during his presentation, he was interrupted by a woman from "the phone room" who asked him to change one of the lakefront lots from "available" to "under contract."

Jack's lips formed a big O, just as I felt mine doing. He leaned over and spit out, "We could buy the one on the lake, put a little house on it and rent it out 'til we retire."

"Yeah, I didn't know they'd be so cheap," I whispered. I was swept into the same dream he was—a warm and distant future for us together. "We can't afford to build now, though."

"Anyway, we can hold onto it as an investment."

"Yeah, let's go for it."

We nabbed the last lakefront lot. They asked us to put two thousand dollars down and agree to small monthly payments.

"Lucky I have my checkbook with me, huh?" Jack said. *An investment in our future,* I thought proudly.

On I-95 in Florida, heading north on the way home, neither one of us spoke. We passed mile after mile of flat, unkempt, scruffy Florida real estate. Menacing sharp fronds. Sand where dirt should have been. Florida would soon be far from our real lives. We'd be back at home and back at work.

I felt slightly sick to my stomach. "I don't know if it was such a good idea to buy property," I said. "Now we'll have these payments on top of our mortgage."

"I know," Jack said, shaking his head. "I've been thinking the same thing."

"Let me see." I dug out the contract from my bag in the back and examined the small print in the paperwork for a path out of the contract.

Fortunately, the State of Florida had the good sense to protect would-be twenty-something landholders with a cancellation clause effective for seventy-eight hours. The next day that sunny version of our future disappeared into the chilly spring air of Long Island.

37.

Walking back into the house after our vacation, I could almost hear the ghosts of our troubles starting to rouse themselves. Memories of the incidents seeped from the doors and tables and walls. *It's different now,* I assured myself. *We remembered how to have fun together.* My energy was renewed, and I felt ready to start actively trying to get pregnant again. That meant putting the special thermometer, the chart, and pencil back on my night table.

We got back to our weekday habit of going to bed around the same time every night, and every night before the lights were out, Jack enveloped me, his hands rubbing and squeezing and fingering me all over, as his invitation to sex.

Late one Thursday night as I was adjusting the covers over me, I said as lightly as possible, "Oh, honey, how about a rain check? We have the whole weekend ahead of us."

Jack sat up and his voice, which had been quiet and breathy, changed sharply. "How the hell are we ever going to get pregnant if we don't have sex?" he said with a force that made me instantly wish I didn't need his help.

"We don't have to do it every day of every month to get pregnant," I said, but it sounded more flip than I intended it to.

"You don't have to teach *me* how it works, " he sneered.

"I'm out of the fertile period now, and we had sex all around the time I was ovulating."

"Well, you're making it a hell of a lot harder for us. You obviously don't want a kid as badly as I do."

"Come on, Jack. That's not fair."

"I'm calling it like I see it," he shouted into my face, and then he threw the covers off and stormed out of the room and down the stairs. I finally fell asleep when it was quiet below and the chill rooted in my body began to fade.

A week or so later Jack announced, "I'm making an appointment for us to go talk to someone."

"Wait a minute. You want to go to therapy?"

"I mean a sex therapist. It won't be just talking therapy. Blah, blah, blah . . . my mother didn't love me, boo hoo. It's about sex, and you gotta admit, there's something wrong with you. It's abnormal not to want sex."

"Let's not go through that again. We're not the same. I don't need sex every single night."

"And that's what a sex therapist can do . . . fix that."

I couldn't muster up a response that wouldn't ignite combustion, so I kept quiet. People were talking more about sex therapy because of Masters and Johnson's popular books on human sexual response, but it sounded creepy to me. "How do you know the person isn't some pervert who wants to get off having people talk about details of their sex acts or, worse yet, watching people have sex?"

"'Cause I got the number from the clinic. They have names. They wouldn't refer me to some charlatan."

"You already have one picked out?"

"Yup, and I'm serious about it too."

The idea of separating our sex issues from the rest of our problems struck me as pointless. But my objections must've sounded to Jack like the cries of a person afraid to deal with "her problems."

The more I thought about it, though, the more I could imagine a positive outcome. Jack was motivated to go. My take on it was that my sex drive was normal, that I was physically attracted to Jack, but he was so needy he couldn't accept me saying "no" to whatever he wanted whenever he wanted it. I guessed that our sex issues would be obvious and the therapist would understand the dynamics. Maybe Jack would listen to what he or she had to say, and that might help us lower the emotional temperature around the topic and find a way to negotiate and compromise.

I was still uncomfortable with the idea, but told him, "All right. Let's try it, but we'll talk it over again after going once or twice."

I relaxed within the first minute of meeting the two people we faced in the cheerful office. The man, a psychologist named Michael, was a balding forty-something with an open face and strong eye contact. His manner was gentle and his voice reassuring.

His female partner, a redheaded social worker named Irene, welcomed us and gave a crisply clear explanation of the various phases in the normal course of treatment. There was nothing kinky, invasive, or voyeuristic. I was pleased when I learned there was to be a lot more discussion about our relationship—communication, trust, and intimacy—than I had expected. We were told we would meet with them, as a couple, a few times and then, as individuals, for a while.

In our first session Irene began by clarifying the definition of a healthy sexual relationship they would be operating under and would be working toward with us.

"No one's needs can dominate the sexual relationship," she said.

Jack startled. "What are you saying there exactly?"

"Well, for sex to be satisfying for a couple, both partners have to be ready to participate."

"But what if one person doesn't want to go along with it?" Jack asked. "Says she's tired." I cringed hearing how he imitated me.

Michael interjected, "Who generally initiates sex in your relationship?"

Jack's lips curved up a bit. "That would be me."

Michael leaned toward Jack. "How do you respond if your wife lets you know she's not interested in having sex then?"

"Well, I touch her where she likes to be touched, use my tongue . . . you know, do whatever I can to get her up for it."

"So you don't accept that she doesn't want to engage in sex at that time."

Jack's demeanor tightened. The conversation wasn't going the way he expected. He was sure he'd already identified the person with the problem.

"Oh, no," he said to them, "You're misunderstanding."

Oh, no. I thought, *they are* not *misunderstanding, God bless them. They understand plenty.* Jack and I did a lot more arguing than having sex during the week between our sessions.

We went for only one more meeting. At the end, Jack announced it wasn't working for him. Michael looked directly into his eyes, shook his hand, and gave him his business card. "Give me a call if you ever change your mind," he told him. "I'd like to work with you."

"Don't count on it," Jack said, but I noticed he put the card in his pocket.

38.

The flicker of hope that sex therapy would help had vanished. It took every ounce of willpower I had to get up in the morning and face the day. I don't know where I'd be now if one particular person hadn't been in Jack's life. I would go so far as to say that she might have been an angel in the guise of a junior high Home Ec. teacher.

Pam was the last person in the world I imagined Jack developing a friendship with at Lincoln. She had been teaching at Lincoln before I arrived, and at thirty-something she was unmarried but dating someone seriously. During my time at the school, I never knew her particularly well. If I had happened to sit at a table with her in the teachers' lunchroom, we might have discussed a recipe for vegetarian lasagna; that was the extent of our friendship. Yet in the years after I left the school, Jack and Pam became close friends.

They got to know each other through their work with the teachers' union. The union was overtaking the pre-existing teachers' association and needed people like Pam, who spoke up for fairness, and people like Jack, who delivered that message with the force of a jackhammer. At some point they began talking to each other about relationship issues. She'd been dating her boyfriend Gordon for several years, but something was holding him back from marrying her while she was ready to settle down and have children. They went to counseling to work this out and eventually married. I never found out how Jack framed our home life to her.

Pam or Jack would periodically arrange things for the four of us to do. It was an unusual experience for me to watch Jack with someone he was so comfortable with. When he spoke, Pam would look directly at him with her brown eyes opened wide. Even if he were saying something outrageous, which he had a talent for, she would listen patiently and smile, maybe make a comment or maybe not. I recognize now that Pam, too, could see something good in Jack beyond his bluster. Often he would come home after one of their talks and quote her to me. It was obvious by the way he talked about her that he trusted her to be thinking of his best interests.

One day following their after-school talk, Jack came into the kitchen as I was cleaning out the coffee pot and sat down at the island. His quietness surprised me, so I put down the sponge and turned around.

"What's up?"

"I was talking to Pam after school about us again." He was measuring his words. "She said their psychologist has really been helping her and Gordon. She thinks I should make an appointment with him for us." I thought I saw his lips tremble.

I hesitated, hearing something I thought I might never hear. I had stopped mentioning the idea of therapy. Coming from my mouth, that suggestion reached him in the form of a grenade. Hope swelled in my chest. I wanted to beg him, Please, please, please, but I said only, "That's a good idea."

"I think so, too," he said. "She gave me his number." Jack picked up his briefcase and walked out of the room and up the stairs.

All that evening we sat side by side on the couch in my room and watched TV. When the last show was over, Jack got up and turned it off. As he headed towards the kitchen, he said, "I'll call tomorrow," and I knew what he meant.

Relief oozed out of every pore in my body—I could have hugged Pam for having the power to make that happen. Therapy held the promise for me that Jack's anger would no longer have the gigantic presence it had. That he would come to understand the dark feelings inside him. That he would be able to talk things out with me. That he wouldn't hurt me anymore.

Dr. Carl Fein's office was on 57th St. in Manhattan. Jack and I drove into the city, in silence, to our first appointment and took seats in a tiny waiting room alongside the patient of another psychologist. I could tell Jack was extremely on edge as though he was an attorney ready to argue the case of his life. Whereas I normally would have caught his nervousness, I thumbed through a magazine and relaxed with the promise of help in the air. It was hard to imagine how anyone could fix our broken marriage, but that hope was with me there in that air-conditioned room with a white-noise box humming away.

Carl was a tall man with curly dark hair, younger than I had guessed, with the slightly bent posture of someone used to ducking under things. With a smile, he extended his long hand to each of us and introduced himself.

I knew from that first moment I walked in that his office was meant for me. I felt like a different, better person in it. Stronger. More like the energetic, optimistic person I had once been. I felt safe with a third person listening to us as part referee, part counselor, part bodyguard. I was sure that Carl would not let Jack's anger take over and cancel me out as it did at home. Carl would be able to see me behind all the garbage that Jack threw, and Jack sure did put out a lot that first day.

"Things would be fine if she were just more sexual," he said.

"You're so demanding and intense about it," I said. "It's not fun."

"That's a lame excuse. You're probably frigid."

We both glanced at Carl, hoping for backup, but when none came I said, "I doubt it. You don't see how you're a big part of . . ."

"What? The problem? Now it's me? I'm the fucking problem?" He leaned in toward me as if to make sure I heard, but he was shouting.

Carl adjusted in his chair. "We're not here to assign blame. We're here to see what each of you has to say about—"

"Well, she's going to give you some convoluted story that's just an excuse." And on it went. His story. His side. And as was always the case, he could not hear one word that might suggest that his take on things was not The Truth without growing louder, angrier, and more panicky.

That sense of panic in Jack's behavior was new that day. Maybe he saw it as his last chance to hold onto his story and protect himself from whatever pain or madness that letting it go would make him feel. I didn't see it like that yet. To me, at our first session, his behavior was simply proof that he was borderline nuts, and I was glad Carl was witnessing it.

I could hardly focus on anything the day after that session. I had spoken more strongly than I did when I was alone with Jack, and he didn't like it. He was agitated, and I was afraid he was going to take it out on me, but he fumed in silence. After a couple of days it wore off, but we never said a word about what went on at our first appointment.

We had three more sessions, but before our fourth session was over, Jack called it quits. Carl was not accepting Jack's assertions that I was the problem and he stormed out in the middle of an exchange, hissing to Carl, "You'll never see me again!"

Jack might as well have started a fire in the middle of the room. What had just happened was too hot for me to acknowledge, so I danced around it for the last minutes.

"I wonder where he is. Maybe he took the car, and I'll have to get a train back."

"How do you feel about going home?"

"I'm not scared really. I expect him to be thinking about what he did. Like he does after he hits me."

"Will I see you next week, with or without Jack?"

"Oh, yes, I'll be here," I said in a voice that could not begin to express the hope I felt. It seemed as if I had never wanted anything more.

39.

When I walked into Carl's office alone for the first time, I took it all in as I hadn't been able to when anticipating Jack's anger. I could feel the nubby texture of the chair's upholstery on my back and legs and the give of the cushion as I sank down in it. I unconsciously stroked the fabric on the wide armrests with my fingertips and felt the cool air on my cheeks. The floor was covered with a patterned Oriental rug and a simple flat couch was on Carl's left. Above the couch were two pictures—simple abstracts, so as not to suggest a narrative. A small pillow showed that a patient's head would be just inches away from Carl. I stared at that couch wondering who laid on it and talked to him. *What do they say?* Sometime later it was me on the couch, but I would not have guessed it then.

Carl and I got into a rhythm in that room. He sat in a black leather chair across from me. Without any hint of emotion on his face, he opened his eyes wide and looked at me. That was my clue that the session was beginning. I heard myself say things that I had been fighting to stifle—"I feel like I'm living in a bad dream." Things I was ashamed to hear—"I don't fight back when he forces himself on me in bed." Things I was glad to hear—"I can't keep living like this." All were things that painted an honest picture of what was going on inside me. It was new to me and glorious to explore them. When I named all the things happening to me, I could no longer pretend they didn't exist.

"Tell me about . . ." he said. "How is it that . . . ?" he asked. I talked and talked about what my life was like, about what was going on with us. I cried. A lot. How could I not? I had felt so alone for years. It was an enormous relief to unload it. No matter what I said, he listened with the same intense interest. He neither used a tape recorder nor wrote down one word, but he often reminded me of details I had mentioned months before, which suggested that he remembered every single thing I ever said.

During most of the session he stayed quiet, which was perfect. The last thing I needed was a man telling me what I should do. He felt my pain, I know, but he didn't show it. After some time with him, I could put words to go along with what I saw in his reactions. When I said, "Jack acts like he's entitled to use me for sex anytime he damn well pleases," I saw his eyes open a little wider. ("Hmm, this is new and important!") Later when I said, ". . . but maybe I should work harder to get myself in the mood," I saw him look down at the floor and adjust himself in his chair. ("Oh! I'd like to shake some sense into her!") But when I said, "I don't owe him anything! It's *my* body!" he fought to hide a smile. ("Yea! She gets it.")

I surprised myself when I once told Carl, "Remember, I was a child who never got hugged."

"Never? That's a strong word."

"Never by my family—neither of my parents. They weren't comfortable hugging. Neither were any of their parents or probably their parents before them. It was me who started giving them hugs after I saw friends at college hugging their parents."

"What does a hug mean to you?"

The words spilled out. "Glad you're alive. I love you. I can't get enough of you."

"Hmm," he said, with a solemnity that shook the walls. Like me, he may have been thinking about a girl who never heard those words or felt their warmth and what kinds of choices that girl might later make.

In the early days of my individual therapy, as soon as I got home Jack asked what I talked about. I struggled to come up with a Jack-approved way of recapping the fifty-minute session. Sometimes I did it successfully and sometimes I didn't. I told him about how I was coming to understand things about myself—where certain behaviors and attitudes came from. Everything I said was true, and most of the time Jack liked hearing about it. After all, it was clear to him that I was the one in our household who needed help.

As I walked into the house one evening with my eyes especially swollen, Jack watched me set down my school bag and take off my jacket. "You had a good session today, I see." It was obvious he wasn't looking for a fight.

"Uh huh. About my father mostly." I blinked furiously, trying to hold the tears in.

"Come here," he said, arms open wide. I moved into him and sobbed with sadness for the little girl inside me. His arms tight around me felt warm and true. *Please, God,* I prayed. *Let it always be like this.*

40.

Those prayers were not answered. Before long Jack started arguing with me about my interpretations of things that had come up in my sessions, as if it were something he could control, should control, as if it were any of his business. One evening, after a good session when I was feeling strong and thinking clearly, I announced, "What went on is for me and me only. From now on I'm keeping it to myself, so don't even ask."

Keeping that balance, though, was harder than I had thought. I couldn't relax when I walked into the house after a therapy session as though I were carrying highly flammable material. I usually stayed quiet and went about the business of getting dinner put together.

One afternoon as I came in, I yelled "Hi," dropped my things onto a chair, and headed into the kitchen. Jack was standing near the sink with a scowl, as if he'd been there for hours waiting to dump on me. *Damn!* Something had gone wrong during the day, and I would have to wallow in its waste. I kept quiet as I opened the refrigerator, poured myself a glass of orange juice, and got out the silverware we needed for dinner.

"Keeping it all to yourself again, huh?" he said. "You are *sooo* happy to leave me out. I can see it on your face." He threw a box of crackers he'd been eating toward me. "Did you two have fun analyzing me?"

How I would have loved to come back to an empty house afterwards! It had been a good session, and I felt raw. I didn't want to get into anything with him, but I couldn't keep it in. "Don't forget, you and I could be working on stuff together," I said, "but *you* walked out."

Jack's face turned fiery red. "Oh, I see. It's *my* fault," he said baring his teeth like a rabid dog. In a flash I felt his knuckles hammer the side of my face. He stamped out of the room and bounded up the stairs. I heard the door click shut.

The anger I felt was stronger than the pain. "I hate you!" I shouted at the ceiling. "You're *impossible!*" I could not believe that I, the person who had just spent fifty minutes in therapy opening up to what was buried inside, was once again getting shut down so brutally. "You *cannot* do this!" I said out loud.

I scurried to the bulletin board hanging next to the phone, looking for the number of the Nassau County police on a list from a realtor. I had never before imagined myself as a person who might need to call the police. But I had noticed it months ago and got the idea.

I dialed the wall phone as quickly as my fingers could move. "Can you send someone over right now? I'm frightened," I murmured. "My husband hit me, and I don't know if it's over."

In the time it took me to fix a bag of ice for my face, two officers knocked on our front door. Jack must have seen them pull up from the upstairs window because he bounded down into the living room as I opened the front door. The pair stepped in as though they were entering a church, holding their hats in their hands in front of them. They took in my puffy eye and my blotchy cheek. The tall one asked, "Are you okay, Ma'am?"

Jack was rigid next to me, our shoulders almost touching. "Well . . . for the time being, " I said, "but he really hurt me and I don't know if he's—"

"Officer, you didn't need to come over," Jack said. "We just had a misunderstanding, but it's cleared up now."

They looked to me for something, but I had no words to explain. His shoulder was touching mine by then. I said only, "This was no misunderstanding." Would these officers ever believe how Jack could pull things out of the air? I saw how police often reported in newspapers that a *fight* had preceded a husband hurting or killing his wife. A *fight*. Yeah, right. Two equally angry people duking it out to claim victory? No, a *fight* is never, ever, how I would describe what happened before I got hurt.

I wanted the police to take charge right away. Weren't they supposed to? The short one said to me, "You need to get an icepack on that eye," then turned to Jack and said, "Look, sir, cool down, all right? You don't need to be doing this." Jack shifted weight from one foot to the other. I felt a balloon grow in my chest and waited.

The two officers looked at each other and then the tall one said to Jack, "Why don't you take your wife out to dinner tonight?"

"I'll do that, sir," he said. They each shook Jack's hand, nodded good-bye to me, and then walked out the door and got into their cruiser. That was it. Five minutes max. The only part that felt right to me was the scared look on Jack's face.

At my insistence he picked up our regular order from the Chinese restaurant, and we ate in silence in front of the television. I pressed an ice pack against my face during the shows. I wanted to make sure he didn't forget why I hadn't cooked dinner.

That night I memorized the police phone number and promised myself I would call again if I needed to. I was hopeful that the next guys might be more forceful. I was certain the police would have to do something if I kept calling, like take Jack in or charge him with something. I could not have imagined then how little protection a woman like me would get from them.

Getting ready for bed that night, I hovered over the bathroom sink, gently splashing water on the swelling under my eye. I brushed my teeth looking down at the drain, not wanting to see the hideousness reflected back in the mirror. I ran my fingers through my hair, not bothering with a brush, and then paused before walking back out to let the reality sink in. In the small bed where our bodies met in the sinking middle, I would be a part of "us" again, no longer "me"—the person who'd gone outside earlier pretending she'd left something in her car, so she could feel the fresh air on her face and sit in the driver's seat, reminding herself it will take her to work, the good part of her life, on Monday.

Stepping into the bedroom I saw Jack focused on a magazine. He knew I'd come in, but he tightened his forehead to appear more attentive to the article. I turned off my light and slipped into my side of the bed with my back to him.

I closed my eyes and lay there, wishing for sleep to come, but knew there would be more. I was sharply aware of everything about Jack— the rustle of paper, his elbow grazing my back, the smell of beer, the in and out of his breath.

Soon his light clicked off. He settled in and his breath slowed. "You okay?" he said.

"Yeah." It didn't matter what the complicated truth was. That was the only answer I could give. Things were better when my mind shut down in bed.

First I felt his warm breath on my shoulder and then his arm encircled me, pulling me close. I didn't flinch or recoil. In fact his touch felt comforting. I reminded myself this was the way he told me he was sorry. We lay there for minutes. Silence. Warmth. Peace.

I was close to sleep when I felt his lips on my neck. Before long two fingers ran gently—very gently—over my breast and down my body. I stroked the fuzz on his forearm. I felt him harden, but I wouldn't turn towards him. So that night we had sex like that, not face to face as we usually did.

That was how sex happened on nights after an *incident*. It always began with gentleness that I understood as a guarantee that it was over. That I was safe, until the next time.

The makeup I'd used to hide my bruise for school had worn off, so I went to my next session with it still colorful. I planted myself in my chair and stared at Carl. I didn't say a word. I let my face do the talking. *See what I let him do to me? See how low I can go?* I felt shame and humiliation, but that day I didn't want to hide with it or from it. My wretched existence would join us there. It was a moment of pure self-hatred, but it would change. I knew my mission in that room was to direct the anger away from me.

"What about going to a neighbor for help?" Carl asked. "It sounds like you know some of the people around you."

"We see them around a lot. The water brings us all outside. Mainly we talk about the weather, or with Jack it's always who caught what out in the bay."

I ran through the houses in my mind. "On one side of us is a couple with four Dobermans and at least one gun. Jack calls the guy Shithead. He and this guy are like two lions on the plains," I said, "They smell something dangerous in each other. When one of the Dobermans gets loose and terrorizes the neighborhood, that's the only time there's any communication between us. Jack stands in our backyard, facing their high fence screaming, 'Get your fucking dog back in the house!'"

Carl fought a smile as I went on. "There's a nice sixty-something couple on the other side of us. He's skinny guy who throws one-liners over the property line. She's a raspy-voiced smoker who rarely comes out of the house. Then across the canal is Jack's fishing buddy Arnie, a really shy guy with a Portuguese wife."

"Do you think your neighbors are aware of Jack's behavior?"

Ah, the question I had asked myself one hundred times. Sound travels on water so it was unbelievable that no one had ever reacted to what went on in our house. Not to Jack's shouts. Not to my screams. Not to me slamming the door to run out front.

"I've always assumed they can't hear us," I said slowly. "I don't know how else to explain why no one, ever once, has tried to help me."

Carl looked down for a few moments before asking, "So, what are you going to do next time?"

I let that question float like a cloud in the air in front of me.

"I have absolutely no idea."

Figuring out what I was going to do felt impossible, but I knew I was in the right place. That was the room that would save me. Or as I understand now, the person I was becoming in that room would save me.

41.

Sitting in the break room at school one morning, nursing a cup of coffee, I listened to the secretaries chattering away. Two of them were nestled in on a couch sharing stories about grandkids.

" . . . so then my son got really angry and said to his three year old, 'Annie, put on *your damn shoes!*' and she said, 'They're not my damn shoes, Daddy, they're my party shoes.'" They squealed at the adorableness of it.

While the two friends one-upped each other with "darling things the kids said," I watched Esther, the sweetest secretary, who was sitting across from them in somber silence. She was looking down at her lap, picking at the donut she held. *Oh, poor thing,* I thought. *I bet it hurts that she has no grandchildren.* At that moment it struck me as so profoundly sad that I started to tear up. I sprang out of my seat and headed to the ladies' room.

I carried my sadness about not being able to get pregnant as if it had nothing to do with my marriage. It was a personal battle—me against my body—that I was losing. Every month when my period came, I felt an insistent drumbeat in my head. What's wrong? What's wrong? What's wrong? It was like a headache that didn't go away and sucked all the joy out of living.

A friend at school was talking one day about a Manhattan fertility specialist her sister had used. His testing went further than that I'd gone through with my assigned gynecologist, and I hoped he might be able to find out what was wrong. I made an appointment and went in to see the doctor.

At my first appointment, he went over my records and gave me an internal exam. He suggested we schedule an endometrial biopsy, where he would snip pieces of the lining of the uterus for testing. It might provide some answers, he said.

On the day of the procedure, I asked about pain medication, but he assured me there was no need—I would feel only a slight tug. A week after the biopsy his office called, but instead of giving me the results, I learned that the doctor had not taken a large enough sample, so I had to go back and repeat the procedure. A tug? It felt more like an evisceration.

Years later, I read an article in a popular women's magazine about this very gynecologist, discussing his respectful ways of dealing with women. The writer highlighted the fact that he gave women the option of having a sheet cover their lower body during an exam. Yet reading about it, all I could think of was how creepy it felt at my first visit with him, when I had sat on the bottom edge of the table with the sheet I had asked for on my lap. The doctor had told me earlier I could keep on my bra, which I soon discovered allowed him, not me, to unhook the snaps in back and with his two hands slide the straps slowly off my shoulders while he watched it fall to my lap and motioned for me to lie back. All the while I had stared ahead at a metal cabinet displaying his smiling family portrait.

But worst of all, despite the pain and indignities, neither biopsy he performed gave me an answer.

"I heard from the doctor today," I told Jack when he came in from work. "He said there's no endometriosis or anything abnormal that would explain it."

He hesitated and then said, "Well, I guess that's good news." But we both knew that it wasn't really good news that something unrecognizable was causing the problem, and it wouldn't be treated. It felt final. I was infertile. It was as heartbreaking as a death. The death of a family, of a life I knew I belonged in.

Without any awareness of my timing, I announced to Jack a week or so afterwards that I wanted to go to the county pound to pick out another cat for us. When I walked along the aisles, peering into cage after cage, I couldn't decide from among the kittens, so I came home with two young females. Jack named one Candy, and I christened the other Clawdia.

Summer came and once again our life revolved around the water. The boat was the best place in the world to be with Jack. He was so proud of it, though it was nothing to look at—nineteen feet of fiberglass dragging a motor, with a console in the middle and a bench. He bought it for the amount of space it had on the sides for him to run along and bring in the fish yanking at his line.

We decided one morning it was a perfect day for us to go out together on the bay. Jack had heard that the stripers were running, and I looked forward to serious sunbathing. The sun was strong but the air was cool.

Standing on the dock, I handed Jack the ice chest and carefully stepped into the boat. He was bending over his rods and tackle box, so I awaited orders from my captain, eager to get through that habitually dicey part of a boat trip with him.

"Turn on the motor," he shouted. "Quick. I gotta get the bait ready . . . Jesus Christ, what'd you do with the chum bucket? . . . Watch out for the rods! . . . Come on, you know, dammit . . . pull out the choke first."

I moved with dizzying speed, but still I heard, "Hurry up, are you going to help or what . . . get the rope . . . no, jerk, leave that one alone . . . this one first!" I did what I was told. I knew the good part was coming.

Jack took the wheel, I freed the boat, and we pulled away from the dock. Gliding along the middle of the canal heading toward open waters, in the fresh salty air with gulls cawing overhead, all was forgiven. The angry barrage was a regular part of boating, and it rolled right off me. After it we became partners, buddies, looking back and forth at each other with smiles on our faces.

We slowly motored along our canal keeping an eye out for neighbors to wave to before Jack cranked up the speed. We couldn't talk with the throb of the motor drowning everything else out. Jack motioned for me to take over the wheel through the deeper waters that led to the bay, while he got his fishing equipment ready. I jumped at the chance to steer; I loved the power pressing against my palms, the rush of air on my face and the speed as we bounced over the choppy waters.

Jack pointed out exactly where he wanted to fish. I listened as he excitedly gave me more information than I cared to have about fluke and weakfish. I directed the boat there, and he took over.

I arranged myself in the narrow aisle to sunbathe, using a rolled-up towel as a pillow. I watched him move his line along the front sides of the boat. His handsome profile. His intense focus. His sure movements. He was competent, in charge and relaxed. I took off my bikini top and covered my arms and chest with lotion. Jack shot a glance my way but turned back toward the deep waters ahead. Nothing else in the world mattered when he was fishing.

I closed my eyes and allowed myself to dream of an ideal life together. I relaxed as pictures spilled out before my eyes. In that fantasy world Jack and I are raising our little girl and boy. I'm at a job in the mornings, but in my room painting in the afternoons. The kids come home, and we sit together in the kitchen and talk and laugh. We work on projects and schoolwork at the table. I prepare healthy, delicious dinners from our garden. Jack comes home, and they follow him into his room. They feed the fish together and tend the plants. They ask him non-stop questions.

On days like this I cannot imagine things will ever get bad again.

I can call up an image of the young woman I was that summer and almost feel what she felt. Alone in the kitchen, she stands by the sink barefoot, always barefoot. A metal blade taps on a wood board as she chops tomatoes for a salad. A cat brushes against her leg. Music that touches her heart plays in the background. The painting she's been working on is propped against the backsplash to dry. It catches her eye and she smiles. The aroma of fish baking in buttery onions surrounds her. She looks out the window at the overflowing garden and sparkling water beyond it. Her man kneels on the dock, intent on untangling some line. Two glasses of flowers she's just cut are lined up along the windowsill in front of her. The late afternoon sun edges them with a fiery glow. She loves where she is and who she is. It's not always like this, she knows. Sometimes it's hard, sometimes it's unspeakable, but it's often like this. Time passes and the memories fade. She feels this is where she belongs. She likes the person she is becoming here.

42.

One rainy morning that summer Jack and I were lounging comfortably close on the living room couch, my legs draped across his lap and two cats nestled between us. One of the kittens scratched at the rug. We were leafing through the Sunday paper after a leisurely morning of sex, with our breakfast coffee nearby, even though it was close to noon. Weekend-morning sex was nice, before his head clouded over with injustices and mine with worry. I put on a Bread album, one of my favorites, and sang along quietly with "Everything I Own." Jack stroked my shin with his fingertips. All was right in our world.

He folded his paper. "What about adopting?" he said, as if we'd been in the middle of a conversation.

Adopting? For a second, I thought he wanted a fifth cat, but looking at his face I understood. It wasn't the first time it had come up, but I recognized that time he was hoping for more than talk.

"You've been thinking a lot about it," I said, not as a question.

"Yeah. I really want to have kids."

"I know you do. So do I. I always imagined I'd have my own kids, but it's looking like that might not happen." I let my chilling words sink in. From the deepest place inside me, I said, "I think you'd be a good father."

All the standard infertility testing was done, and the doctors had found no reason why I wasn't able to get pregnant. But adopting . . . that scared me. Opening up our life to Social Services? People who would look for and expect something I couldn't promise? But I knew that adopting wasn't something that happened quickly. There was always a wait, usually a couple of years, before a baby would become available, and that was only if you made it onto their long list.

So that day, alongside Jack's warm body, I said, "Let's give it a shot." The next day I called the county Social Services and by the end of the following week we had their adoption forms.

That was a route filled with landmines. Things all along that path kept both Jack and me on guard. Easy, first-page questions challenged us—"What is your religion?" is a sticky one for Baptist/Catholic non-church-goers.

There were worse questions, ones we knew we would be strictly judged on. Things like, what makes your marriage work? What will be your strengths and weaknesses as parents?

I remember clearly the photo of us that we had to submit along with the application. We had asked Jack's brother Brian to take it, but we were the ones who carefully orchestrated it. I am sitting in our antique rocking chair, very erect, in a crewneck sweater. Jack is standing behind me, straining to be as tall as possible, with his two hands on my shoulders. He and I look directly into the camera. We are both attempting smiles, though our expressions are unreadable, quite like the farm couple in the painting, *American Gothic*. On the wall behind us is an oak regulator clock we bought in the Amish country. We were presenting ourselves as a serious, traditional couple, maybe even a little old-fashioned.

The week after we finalized the application process, I brought it up in my session with Carl, telling him all that was involved and how we answered the questions. I hadn't mentioned it in therapy before and stayed away from my feelings about having a child with Jack that seesawed depending on my sense of comfort at home.

"You're eager to have a baby with Jack," he said, with no special emphasis or hint of emotion.

"Well, I wouldn't exactly say 'eager'." I understood he was throwing in "with Jack" as if I needed reminding. "And everyone tells me it takes a long time before you get a child—at least a year, maybe two or three . . . and that's if they approve you as suitable parents."

"Is that a concern?"

"No, not really," I said, immediately realizing I needed to convince myself that was true. "Jack's very much into the adoption route, and they could see that when they interviewed us . . . he was good when they visited the house."

"So he was good for them."

"I can see what you're getting at, but yes, damn it, yes." I decided not to tell him that a part of me was always prepared to have the agency reject us at any minute. "I'm going ahead with the application for now. I don't know, okay? I don't know anything for sure but I'm going along with it."

He didn't need to say aloud, "So you're *going along with* it." I was hearing that truth loudly and clearly in my mind. Once the application and interview process were completed, there was a long silence from the agency. I was glad because I didn't want to talk about it in my sessions any more. Ambivalence is strikingly transparent in therapy.

43.

One night in early fall I watched Jack and his dad unload the boat from our kitchen window. Timmy was inspecting the fish in the buckets. They weren't saying a word to each other. His dad and Timmy walked along the side of the house carrying all their things directly toward their car. I was surprised; Timmy usually stopped in so he could fill me in on the day's catch and maybe find something on the kitchen counter to nibble on. I dreaded that something had gone wrong.

Jack set his bucket of fish down outside and tramped in, boots and all. A fishy, sweaty smell followed him.

"The damn fuel line's not clean," he bellowed as he sat at the counter taking off his boots. "She kept stalling. It took us so fucking long to get back." I turned on a low heat under a pot, as he slid out of his rain gear.

"Somebody must've put some goddamn gunk into the gas tank!"

"Not so loud, please," I said. "I feel like you're angry at me." I stood at the stove stirring the sauce.

"I am angry. Angry at you 'cause I'm not getting any support here."

"That's not true. I'm warming up dinner. I'm sorry it happened, but let it go for tonight. Deal with—"

"I can't just forget about things and make them go away like you can." His voice sent electric currents through me.

"That's not fair. It's not me. You're pissed off 'cause the boat has—"

"*Wrong!* I'm pissed off 'cause I have a wife who doesn't take my problems seriously."

"That's crazy, Jack. I—" but I didn't get another word out, before I jerked to the right to avoid a thick glass mug he'd launched toward me, barely missing my head. It clipped a cabinet then hit the floor with a thud.

"That could have killed me!" I screamed. His face scared me. He threw that mug like a spear in the jungle. His hand moved along the counter. I had to get out fast.

"You were asking for it, getting wise . . ." I heard him say as I ran to the back door barefoot and knocked it open. Feeling like an animal running for its life, I dashed toward my car by the curb, opened the door, sprung into the back and pushed the locks in one quick motion. Catching my breath, I looked up and all around. Jack was nowhere I could see, so I knelt on the backseat and curled up in a ball as tightly as I could.

It was quiet outside. Crickets serenaded as if I were sitting on a porch in a glider with a cup of tea. I was safe there, and I promised myself I'd stay there forever if I had to. I hugged myself as my breath slowed.

SMACK! A thud by my head. The car shook. I looked up, and Jack's face was only inches from mine, distorted against the rear window. "Grrrrr!" he roared as his two open hands pushed against the glass. I opened my mouth, but nothing came out. Again, I tried to scream. Jack stepped back and laughed an "I-gotcha" laugh as if we were kids playing a game.

"Come back in. Don't make such a big deal," he said. "Sorry I was pissed."

That night I crawled into my side of the bed after he'd gone to sleep. All I could think was that he'd scared me so much I couldn't have called out "Help!" if he'd come in after me. I lay in the darkness staring at the ceiling with my eyes wide open.

In therapy Carl made sure I knew that my safety was the most important thing. He questioned me about that as he had about other *incidents* until I shouted, "He could have killed me!" He wanted those words in the room, with their acrid odor.

"So you're choosing to stay in a very dangerous place," he said.

"It's not like I can just go live someplace else!"

He ignored my delivery. "I wasn't thinking about you living someplace else. I meant what about you going someplace else whenever you feel in danger."

I absorbed the possibility of getting to a safe place for a night. Not packing a bag and walking out for good on shaky feet, but rather, every time I was hit or didn't feel safe, getting out of the house. But where could I go?

During the evening later that month, as the final gesture of his latest tirade, Jack pushed me into the corner of the kitchen counter and I tumbled to the floor. When I heard him go upstairs, I snuck out of the house to my car and headed fifteen minutes north to his family's house. I didn't call them. I simply drove up, parked out front, and knocked on the door as if I weren't afraid this might somehow backfire.

His mother clenched her jaw when she saw that it was me alone at the door. "What's wrong?" she said right away, not "Hi" or "Come on in." I took it to mean she had been expecting me one day.

"I'm sorry to do this to you," I said, unable to stop myself from apologizing. "I had to get away fast. Jack's on a rampage and I'm scared. He pushed me, and my back hurts."

"Let me see," she said. I turned around and lifted my sweatshirt. "Uh, it's red and starting to swell. Let me get some ice."

"No, it'll be okay. Listen, can I stay here tonight?" I asked. By then the two girls were standing behind her.

Jean surprised me with her quick reaction. "Diane, you stay in with Julie tonight," she said, "and go get what you need from your room right now."

I exhaled deeply. I'd been afraid they'd want to know details, and I didn't want to stand for another minute at the door.

"Diane's room," she said and tilted her head in that direction.

After a couple of minutes in the bathroom, I climbed into bed in my T-shirt and underpants and folded into a fetal position, willing sleep to drown me.

Fifteen minutes later, though, I heard Jack's van pull up in front, tires screeching. They must have called him. I couldn't catch a breath when I heard him bark at the front door, "Where is she?" I braced for the pounding I expected to hear on the stairs, but none came. I stayed perfectly still up in bed.

For the next hour I could hear shouting in the kitchen. I couldn't decipher most of what he was saying, and I didn't want to. I wondered if any of them could see through what he must have been reporting about me. I was just thankful they were not letting him come up, and when the clamor stopped, I heard his car drive away.

"I feel trapped," I told Carl at my next session. "They didn't do anything. But what could they do? He's impossible."

"Where can you go to get safe next time? To your friend Lynn's?"

"I can't do that." I shook my head, taking time to make sure that was true. "I can't go barging in, waking them up at night. They have to get up for work." I was breathing fast as I blurted out, "What if Jack figured out where I am, comes over, and goes nuts on them?" Carl didn't say anything. We were probably both imagining it.

"I'd be so ashamed."

Carl looked down and adjusted the leg of his pants. I knew that pause in our back-and-forth was for special emphasis on what he was about to say. "Well, then," he said, "What about going to a motel for the night?"

"Me? Go to a motel?" I had to let that sink in. "A motel? . . . Maybe . . . Somewhere between home and work."

"Yes, just get yourself to a safe place." He paused to let me absorb it, then added, "And do it every time you don't feel safe."

44.

As the school day ended and the guidance suite cleared out, I got into the habit of stopping by my friend Maxine's office to see if she was free. She had a reputation among the administrators for being too casual about the ever-present paperwork and keeping track of which students were her responsibility. Yet I had noticed when students came to her with a personal problem, she would close her door and talk with them for an hour sometimes. Those students would come back again and again to work with her, and the bond she had with them was almost visible. I found from her the same level of attention and interest she showed to students with serious problems. When she talked to me about the negative evaluations she'd gotten for not keeping up with busy work, I told her she should have been a therapist rather than a high school counselor in a bustling office.

In our after-school talks, she told me about the arguments that arose in her household between her husband, Sid, a leader in the county teachers' union, and her son from an earlier marriage. I eased into conversations about Jack and me. She had met him at social events, where he drank more than usual and came up with provocative statements that got the younger guys laughing and egging him on while the rest of us watched tight-lipped. She had the right instinct to keep quiet with me about her impressions of him. With no need to defend myself, I opened up about my marriage.

"Most times I have no warning when it's going to happen," I told her, "When something is going to trigger that thing inside him that makes him explode."

"Then he lashes out at you. Hits you even."

"Yeah, he can't control himself. He's not looking at me like his wife. He's looking at me like I'm Evil personified."

"Then he hurts you."

"Uh huh. Badly sometimes."

She said nothing, barely shaking her head.

I had been in therapy for almost two years by then, but I wasn't yet aware of the power it was having on the way I thought about myself. It was introducing me to the person I am after I shake off all the lessons I carried from others about who I am and who I should be.

And therapy can be underhanded. You think you're there to work on a specific problem, like living with an abusive husband, but all sorts of seemingly unrelated things come out, and that's where the clues are. I would start recounting something that took place with Jack when suddenly I would start unearthing a story from the 1950s as if it had happened yesterday.

One such story that came out resonated for all the sessions that followed, though at first when I told it, I didn't have any idea that it held such power. When I heard myself saying, "I remember . . . " I wasn't sure if I was telling the truth. But in that silent room, staring out at the sky over the city, I spoke without hesitation, and it seemed incredible that I was remembering something so clearly that occurred when I was four years old.

We were in the dining room of our tiny row house in Philadelphia. The table and chairs barely fit in the room, and adults had to hold in their breath as they circled around to set or clear the table.

That day we had company—my father's parents and my Aunt Helen. My father sat at the head of the table with his back to the window. When we were finished eating and the grown-ups were talking. I got down from my chair and jumped up on the side rung of his. He looked so big and handsome that I reached up for my daddy to sit on his lap. As soon as I touched him though, he flinched and twisted away. His cheeks turned bright red, and he stammered as he elbowed me away. "Get off me. Get down."

It shocked me—the painful push, his harsh words and the look on his face I didn't yet recognize as embarrassment.

I'm sure that wasn't the first time I had been rejected so definitively, but I probably made it the last. Carl would call up that incident for me many months after I mentioned it, and if he saw me these decades later, I feel he would still see in my eyes what registered on my four-year-old face that day.

45.

A scene on a night that winter of '75 plays out in my mind as clearly as a film running before my eyes.

I am standing alone in the downstairs room I claimed for myself. It's after eleven, and outside it's black and still. I hear the last of Jack's footsteps on the stairs, and then the door slams shut. My ears are still ringing. Jack was on a tear, furious about something at school. He recounted what happened again and again, slightly altering each version to sharpen his point or, as it sometimes seemed, to discover details that could stir him up even more as if that were his goal. Every single thing I said to him was wrong.

"You just want me to shut up," he said, "You don't give a shit."

Now alone in my room, my jaw, where his hand punched it, throbs with pain. For all I know he and I may have been in there earlier that night, laughing together as Archie Bunker and Meathead were squaring off. Things could turn upside down in an instant.

I'm in my room for its emptiness and its silence, thankful that I have a place to settle myself down and think. His words knocked all thoughts out of my head.

All I want to do is curl up on the couch and grab a pillow to hug. I move toward it, but something keeps me standing. This time I don't want to sit down. I don't want to get more comfortable in this house. Who knows what waits for me upstairs? I stare out the window at the blackness. There's frost on the panes where the cold meets the heat. Nothing is moving on our street. Most houses are dark; everyone's gone to bed, and I am so, so tired.

A shiver runs through me, and my body holds onto the chill. I know I'm in a warm house, in my cozy room with its sofa and books and TV, but looking out into the night, I feel as frightened as if I were standing alone on an ice floe in the black Arctic night.

I can't go out. Not now, I think. Where would I go? I take long, slow breaths and cross my arms tight against my chest as though I'm hugging myself.

I turn out the light next to the couch and take my long winter coat from the closet. Without a sound I grab my keys from the kitchen counter and slide the back door open barely wide enough for me to fit through sideways. I whisper "Good-bye" to Isabelle who has followed me. Then I dash alongside the house and get in my car at the curb.

As if I have just awakened, I am sharply aware that I'm sitting there in the driver's seat of my car, with my hands clutching the wheel and directing it where to go. I drive to the end of our block and turn right, heading east to the Holiday Inn.

The next day after school Jack said he was sorry he got so upset. He'd had a bad day. He hugged me and planted a kiss on my cheek, above my bruise. He didn't try to come up with an explanation to bridge the gap between having a bad day and almost breaking my jaw. My side of the bed had stayed cold again, and he was chastened, noticeably careful around me for the next days.

Something more dramatic had changed for me though. Leaving that night gave me power, not over him, but as insignificant as it might sound, the power to see us more clearly than ever before as two separate people.

Part 3

46.

Jack and I hadn't heard from the county adoption agency for months. I thought about it from time to time but didn't pick up the phone to inquire. I wasn't eager to revisit the anxiety that topic created between us. Finally in March, at Jack's insistence, I called the office.

"Can you tell me anything about the progress of our application?" I asked the assistant at the desk. She put me on hold and didn't get back to me for a while. I tried to imagine how many couples they were dealing with. Did she have to sort through twenty-five files? One hundred? More? She clicked off Hold and cleared her throat. "I found your file," she said. "I'm sorry, but you're no longer in our 'active pile.'"

"What does that mean?" I said, with more curiosity than distress.

"Well, one criterion we have for judging couples is how persevering they are. We haven't heard from you for six months or so."

She may have expected me to leap in with excuses, justifications, or explanations for our restraint, but instead I asked her not to remove our file completely and thanked her. I didn't feel ready to take out adoption as an option, but I wasn't going to push it along either.

When Jack asked about the call, I said only, "She told me it's in the works."

One weekend in early spring, while I was dusting the downstairs and straightening up, Jack paced behind me growling about something that had happened with Ed the day before at school. I was busy doing something I wanted to finish quickly so I could go shopping with Lynn at Roosevelt Field. His angry words hit me like pellets, and I didn't want to hear one more word.

"Jack, please. I really, really wish you could let go of this."

"Just hear me out," he said, and without missing a beat kept going. "You won't believe how he could turn something I said into . . . "

If only, I thought for the one-hundredth time, *if only he were talking to his own therapist about these things that drive him nuts.*

A few months before I had given him a new wallet for his birthday, and as he transferred things from his old one into it, I was shocked to see he had saved the business card of the sex therapist Michael. I remembered their exchange as we left our last session and assumed Jack would have tossed it. The fact he had saved it gave me something to wrap my hope around. Yet on his birthday I'd been afraid to mention it. Therapy was one of those words that ignited his fires like a match to gas.

That Saturday morning I decided to bring it up. "Jack, listen for a second," I said nervously twisting my dust rag, "I'm worried this thing with Ed is upsetting you too much."

"What do you mean, 'upsetting me too much'? How do you know how I feel?"

"I don't know how you feel, but I hate seeing you carrying it around and ruining your day off."

"So, what exactly are you saying?"

"I know what a relief it is to talk things out with Carl so maybe . . ."

"I'm not stepping a foot back in that fucking office—"

"I wasn't going to say that. What about calling up Michael, that sex therapist, and talking some of these things out?"

"What the hell could he do? It's not like he could make that asshole stop trying to . . . "

Again that door slammed shut as forcibly as if a gust had blown in.

I had started carrying my camera with me most of the time since I was taking an evening photography class. So later that month as I organized the closet in my den, I sorted through black and white prints I'd done for class. I separated the landscape and still life shots, lining up the best ones along the bookshelf to find two to hang together.

As I worked that day, I could hear Jack rustling around in the kitchen, so I decided to take a break for lunch. From the hall I saw him hunched over a pile of papers with his elbows on the counter, fingers combing through his hair, and schoolbooks scattered all over. His tension smacked me in the chest. *Keep it light,* a voice in my head whispered.

"I'm going through my photos from last semester to find a couple to hang up." When I talked about art projects, my words tumbled out. "I really loved that class. I learned so much about composition from all the critiquing." I grabbed some lunchmeat and bread from the refrigerator and started to put together a sandwich by the sink.

"Pictures from the class you took with that stud, what's-his-name, you told Lynn about?"

"He was hardly a stud," I said, surprised he had remembered something I had said to Lynn. "I just said he was nice-looking for an older guy."

"Looks to me like you're taking those courses just to sniff around like a bitch in heat," he said, now up and coming toward me. He pinched my buttocks hard.

"Ouch, damn it. That hurt." I said rubbing my rear. I swung around to see if his face told me what was going on, and I didn't like what I saw. *Go easy here,* I was thinking. "Trust me," I said forcing a smile. "I'm not after any fifty-year old."

"Why, you like them younger? Huh?" He pushed my shoulders with both hands and my back banged against the sink. "Huh? How old was Ted? Twenty-eight? Twenty-nine? You like them young, huh?" he breathed onto my face.

I could feel the black energy building in him, and I needed some space between us quick. I stepped away from the sink and counter, but he moved right along with me. "Jack, come on. What's going on now?" I touched his arm as a peace offering.

"Don't fucking touch me, whore." His face was as white as I'd ever seen it. I spun around and ran down the hall to my room, slamming the door. I was sure there was a lock, but there wasn't. I pushed my back against the door with unexpected force, but the weight of his body swung it open as if I weren't there.

It's over, I thought. *This is it.*

In a primal move I fell to my knees and curled into the tightest ball I could. I shut my eyes and covered my head with my hands waiting for the pain to start. He kicked my hip with his bare foot. "You can't get away from me," he growled and, pronouncing each word with a kick, he said, "Don't. Even. Think. It."

The air swirled around me, so I knew he walked out of the room. I stayed as small as I could until I heard the back door open and shut. My left side was sore, but I rolled over and sat up with my back against the couch.

Kicking me? Like an angry kid? I thought. *He's never done anything like that.* I stared at the wall in front of me to let my mind form words to explain the idea that was forming. No matter what he'd just said or done, it didn't land on me like anger, but something less scary, more like aggravation than rage. Then it came to me that what I felt from him was frustration. The simple truth was, I decided that day, he thinks he's losing me and doesn't know what the hell to do about it.

47.

In therapy during my sessions that April, I listened to myself as my talk bounced off Carl. He repeated words, even sentences, I had said to let me hear what had come out of my mouth, and as he intended, those words stayed with me long after the session was over. As I felt myself come back into my body, I heard what I had already decided to do.

In one session I summed it up for myself. "I hate to say it but it's the sad truth. No one can help me. I'm not safe in my own goddamn house, and it's me who has to do something about it."

"No one's going to help you," he said with a nod. "You're not safe and you're the only one who can change that." I could see then that he'd been waiting a long time for me to say those words.

That frightening reality was not easy to hear. Once I had told Carl sharply, "You know what I should do and you won't tell me." He looked right back at me and said nothing. That made me wail, "You're making this so hard for me. It's infuriating!" He stayed quiet and let me hear the lone voice in the room. I came to understand what it was that I was screaming—"I know what I have to do, but I have no idea how to do it."

How could Carl know what was possible for me to do? For all he knew if I left without having a plan and support in place, Jack could pressure me into coming back and make it even worse for me. Or, for all he knew, Jack might find me and hurt me or kill me. We all knew of men who did that and the thought of it had paralyzed me.

I remember one session so clearly from those months. I cried out,

"How am I ever going to get out of this? What has to happen to get me ready to do it? I know it's what I should do."

"*Should* do?"

"Okay, okay, I get it, but you know what I mean . . . want to do . . . I have to get out of this marriage . . . I just don't know how on God's earth I can get away . . . escape . . . that's really the right word. Escape."

"You know Paul Simon's song, 'Fifty Ways to Leave Your Lover'?"

"Of course."

"Well, I don't know how you'll do it, but maybe now that you've started leaving to get safe for a night or day, here and there, you'll tire of that and you'll come up with one of those fifty ways to stay away for good."

From then on that melody lurched around my head like a record with a scratch.

Sometime later Carl asked. "What's stopping you from packing a bag tomorrow and not going home?"

"Are you kidding? Jack would be up at my school the next day. I can't imagine what he'd do. I don't think he'd get violent—at least not at first. I could be sitting there talking to one of my kids and see his face in the window of my office. He'd look crazed. I'd probably faint. But he'd insist on talking to me. I'd try to tell him, 'Not now. Later,' but he'd refuse to leave. All the kids would be watching. The people I work with would try to calm him down, and that would really piss him off. He'd start yelling. He'd try to get people on his side. It would be a nightmare. I can't imagine how it would end either." I struggled to catch my breath as I felt myself shrivel into one raw nerve.

Carl sat quietly waiting for more.

"You're probably thinking the police could be called but, oh my God, can you imagine? The police coming into my school with everyone around watching? No, no. I can't do it."

We both let that settle in. "So it would be difficult to leave while school is in session," he said after a while.

A short summary of what I had rambled on about—that was

his magic. That was all it took for me to understand when I got the strength to leave, I wouldn't jeopardize the job I loved. It meant I would leave that summer.

48.

During the weeks that followed I had a recurring dream. I stayed in bed as long as I could to keep the feelings with me. *I am running down our little street away from the house, past the big house next door with the barking Dobermans, past the little white house with black shutters, past the tan house with the weedy lawn, over the cracks in the sidewalk, toward the busy street at the end of the block. My breath is deep. My legs feel strong and sure. My head is clear and a smile is on my face. As I swing my arms and take in the cool, fresh air I feel powerful and free. When I get to the end of the block, I look both ways and realize that I can go anywhere I want.*

On weekends that spring, come rain or shine, Jack went out on the boat with one of his brothers. He left as soon as he got up and didn't come back until late afternoon. One Sunday it was unseasonably warm, so I put an album on the turntable, grabbed my book, and settled down outside on a lounge chair. The cats were hunting in the gardens around me, and one batted at a grasshopper.

Before long I noticed I was re-reading every paragraph a couple of times because something else wanted my attention. Pictures flashing behind my eyes. A bright, empty room waiting to be filled. Shiny parquet floor. Freshly-painted walls. I could see myself putting a container with bright red begonias on a windowsill, placing a small table and chairs by it, where I could sit to eat while I looked out at the city streets below. It would be my place, the quiet place where I could be alone with my favorite things. Against a wall across from my bed would go the unfinished antique oak chest we bought in Pennsylvania with delicate carving and brass pulls.

When I heard the voices of Crosby, Stills, Nash and Young float out the window, "Our house, is a very, very, very fine house / With two cats in the yard . . . " My eyes burned with tears. Jack and I called it "our song." It was us at our best. How could I think about leaving this place, this man, this family, my furry babies, this life that I built?

As the sun went down, Jack came home, sunburned and smelling of the sea, so proud of the boatload of fish he and our neighbor Arnie had caught. He had cleaned them outside and picked out a big one for me to fix up for the broiler. I heard loud laughter out back and looked into the darkening yard. I could see the two of them, sitting back in lounge chairs, legs out in all directions. Arnie said something to Jack who let out a guffaw. He looked like king of the manor with his cigar raised and the smoke winding through a ray of light from the kitchen. I want him to always be this happy.

While Jack took a shower that night, I sat in bed reading. I could smell English Leather as soon as he stepped into the bedroom with his hair still dripping and an impish smile. How clever he was, playing to my weakness for that aftershave.

All the same, I spent hours the next weekend in the garage, putting coats of stain on my oak chest to give it new life.

49.

I told Carl at my next session, "My friend Pam suggested I go to the infertility specialty clinic in the city where she and her husband went through a work-up." Carl looked at the floor and shifted around in his chair. I could only imagine now how it must have sounded for me, who'd been talking about leaving her husband, to be talking about pregnancy.

"They're so motivated to have a baby," I said, "so I'm sure she's looked for the best fertility expert in New York."

"And you're also so motivated to have a baby," he said like a statement of incontestable fact.

"Yes," I said with emphasis. "I want so badly to have a baby." I paused. "Someday." I gathered strength as I said the words out loud. "I'm desperate to know what's going on with me. My body's not working right, and I want to know if anybody can figure it out. I want to have kids."

Carl stayed quiet instead of pointing out everything I already knew about how questionable my timing was.

I made an appointment at the clinic Pam suggested for later that month and went in for the informational appointment alone. The elderly specialist, Dr. Denton, who had founded the practice, looked like a diminutive mad scientist, but his reputation and promise made him look like a god to me. I sat across from him at his messy desk as he looked through the packet of information I had brought. He spent more time than I'd expected reviewing my records, and then announced that the only test still needed was the one he was known for—a procedure called a culdoscopy that would allow him take a microscopic look at my reproductive organs.

The day of the procedure Jack and I took off from school. He drove me into the city and waited to take me home since I needed to be sedated. The test required me to get into the most convoluted position—on my knees with my rear end skyward—but I would have stood on my head for that doctor. Through a slit in my vaginal wall, he viewed my ovaries, uterus, and tubes mid-cycle with an instrument that took pictures and sample cells.

While I rested in the post-op room, the doctor came by. He said that the procedure went well, and I should hear from his office in a week or so to schedule the follow-up appointment. He asked for my permission to share with his students the photos his instrument was able to take of my organs. I was too groggy to ask why, but the next day I was encouraged that maybe he'd observed something meaningful. A day later I was discouraged thinking maybe something was so wrong it should be documented. A long week followed.

I drove into that appointment alone with an active mix of excitement and fear. In his office, excitement took over as soon as I heard the words, "I was able to find . . ." Dr. Denton told me he had diagnosed a chemical problem with the luteal phase of my cycle. I bombarded him with questions, and he went through a full explanation of that phase, the one that comes after ovulation. The relatively new drug, Clomid, might eventually work, he determined, so he gave me a prescription for five tablets with clear instructions. No vaginal sex for one month, he said, then begin taking the pills after a second month to allow for healing, one pill each night at the start of a menstrual cycle.

That was the first time a gynecologist had suggested something. He said it "might work" not "will work." I got the prescription filled and put it in the medicine cabinet. I liked knowing the pills were there. Some days during those months I swore I would never touch them, but on other days I thought I might try.

I understand now, when it came to having a baby, I had a gigantic blind spot.

One cloudy Saturday in June, Jack bounded into the kitchen from the yard. He yelled into the living room where I was making piles of his magazines and papers. The room was an extra mess from the final exams he'd finished correcting along with the answer sheets, last-minute homework, and administrative instructions.

"What did you do with my fishing knife?" He appeared at the doorway where he had a look that implied I had a hell of a nerve moving his things around.

"Nothing. I haven't seen it for a while." I fluffed the couch pillows since the cats had jumped off and darted away at his booming voice.

"You must have used it for something. Think. Think," he snarled, drumming his fist against the side of his own head as though he were illustrating what he'd like to do to my head.

"Sorry, Jack," I said calmly. "I didn't touch it. You'll find it somewhere." Hoping to change the subject, I was just about to ask if he wanted to go to the movies later, but he charged toward the plant room.

As much as I wanted to distance myself from his anger, I couldn't stop my guts from churning. His energy filled the air as he ricocheted around the downstairs, fingering every surface, grumbling more than yelling. When he finally stopped, I sighed loudly. The house was quiet again. *The less engaged I am, the better,* I decided.

Jack walked back into the living room, passing by me as he headed to the foot of the stairs. *He must have given up,* I thought. Pleased he was getting out of my way, I relaxed as I dusted the end table under the stairs. He had one foot on the bottom step when he turned to me and stared. I froze when I noticed his tight lips. In a flash he struck me with a boulder-like fist on the side of my head, an inch from my eye. I shrieked. He clambered up the stairs and slammed the door.

I was aware of that moment as if I were looking at myself from a distance, from the point of view of another person. He—that man, my husband—had decided to hurt me badly for something that had nothing to do with me. That punch, that searing pain to my temple that seemed to have come out of nowhere didn't really come from "nowhere." It had come out of him and a convoluted choice he made to hurt me, I told myself. He could not or would not make himself stop. What if he had hit an artery or something? He could've killed me.

From that moment on, I couldn't shake the thought, how much longer will I let him do this?

50.

On the mild Friday morning before the Fourth of July weekend, Jack and I were both at home, in and out of the house taking care of things that had been ignored during the busy final weeks of the school year.

I was on my knees in the bathroom rinsing out the tub I'd just scrubbed. In the background was Jimi Hendrix's "Purple Haze," a version that seemed to go on and on without end.

I felt Jack burst in. "Goddammit," he yelled, with the tile doubling the volume.

I jumped to my feet and faced him with my legs pressed against the tub, a sponge in one hand and Ajax in the other. There was barely enough room for the two of us in there.

"What's wrong?" I asked. We were inches apart. I felt I was hearing his heartbeat.

"A whole damn tray of seedlings is dying! You must've moved them out of the light."

"I hardly ever go in that room. You know that."

"Of course you don't. You wouldn't give a shit about what's important to me. This is just one more thing that shows you . . . " and on and on it went. His accusations got louder, bouncing off the walls, almost in rhythm with Jimi's voice. His body blocked the door.

"Jack, stop for a minute," I said calmly, wanting to change where this was going, but his face knotted up.

"Stop?" he said gritting his teeth. "Stop? I haven't started," and with that he drilled three punches into my upper arm that stung like a branding iron. Isabelle meowed from under the sink.

My arm was on fire. I threw down the cleaners and sat on the edge of the tub. "Go! Get the hell outta here."

Jack walked out of the room more slowly that I had expected. He turned to glance at me and then disappeared behind the wall. I imagined he was thinking about what he'd just done. Regretting it. *Goody for him*, I thought, *but it's too fucking late. I can't believe I took my third Clomid last night. How could I ever think of having his kids!* Those punches certainly weren't the worst thing he'd ever done. I wouldn't need to go to the hospital or call the police. I wouldn't need to escape to his parents' house or find a motel. I wouldn't even bother covering the bruises with make-up. No, this wasn't the worst thing he'd done, but sitting there on the bathtub, I swore to myself it was the last thing I would ever let him do to me.

I didn't move for minutes. I was full of an energy too big to name. I knew that from that moment on his issues, his anger, would be *his* problem not mine. "That's it!" I said out loud so I could hear it float in the air in front of me. "I'm going."

I stood up, opened the medicine cabinet, and picked up the orange pill container. I squeezed it hard as I stared through it. Then it came to me: the doctor gave me what I've been aching for—hope that I might someday be a mother. I twisted off the lid and dumped the last two Clomid pills into the toilet. I flushed, watched the swirl and walked out of the little purple room.

51.

The power I felt that day was so forceful, I imagine now that if I hadn't heard Jack start his car at the curb and pull away, I might have simply walked out of the house and kept on going. But he was avoiding me, so I could stay right there and absorb what I had promised myself. I went out back and sat on a railroad tie along a flowerbed, as I'd done a hundred times before. I let my hands move restlessly to find little weeds to pull. I looked around at the beds already filling with flowering plants. Then I remembered: the next day the yard would be full of people.

We had been making our usual plans for a holiday weekend with Jack's family. They'd be over on Saturday to go out on the water. On Sunday the Fourth we all planned to go on the boat, have dinner at our place, and then go back out and watch the fireworks on the bay. After all it was not just any Fourth of July weekend. It was America's Bicentennial, and celebration plans had been in the works for years all around the country.

I had to go ahead, no, I *wanted* to go ahead with the weekend plans, even though it would be so hard to be with his family. I'd have to muster all the courage I could find to be around those kids, wondering if I might ever see them again. But I couldn't for a second let on to what is going on inside me.

A plan formed in my head spontaneously, as if it had been tucked in there all along. *Give yourself some time to prepare. Drive into the city to next Thursday's therapy appointment. Have the session but don't come home. Keep driving out on the Island to Babylon and stay with Maxine and her husband.*

Just thinking about the new safe place I'd found made me feel more determined. During one of our afternoon talks at school, Maxine had leaned toward me and said, "You know anytime you need to, you can come stay with us." She covered my hand with hers. "I mean that." On the last day of school she had made a point of telling me they'd be home until the middle of August.

Somehow I found a way to go through the motions on Saturday without sending off any signal that I carried a bombshell on my back. I was on emotional overload that weekend, so it surprises me now how I can bring back a scene from Sunday the Fourth so clearly.

I'm in the kitchen, wearing denim shorts and a halter-top, standing barefoot on the sticky linoleum floor at the butcher-block that juts across its middle. On the wood slab are the ingredients for my baked clams that Jack and his family always beg me to make. He and Timmy got me the clams the old fashioned way, walking barefoot at the good beaches they knew and curling their toes in the sandy low waters until they felt the ridged shells. They brought home their bounty and shucked them. I mince the clams and slice the onions and chop the parsley and press the garlic with unusual vigor. All of me is going into those clams I'm making for them: my love, my fear, my guilt. The loss.

That afternoon everyone except me went out on the water to see the tall-masted ships from all over the world parade across New York Harbor for Operation Sail. I know what transpired on that weekend only from TV and magazines I saw later. I'm aware that hot air balloons hovered overhead. Hundreds of small boats floated nearby for a look at the majestic crafts. People with connections stood at the narrow windows high up in the World Trade Towers for the best views.

To be out on the water with Jack and his family would have been impossible for me. To be surrounded by their excitement, their questions, their quibbling, but mostly, their heartbreaking ignorance would've been too much to bear, so I had told them I needed more time to fix dinner.

I went outside and sat on the lounger under the mimosa, the only tree on our property. "Betty's tree," Jack called it, since it was my favorite spot to read and relax. Seagulls squawked. A small motorboat went by pulling a boy on an inner tube. People up and down the canal were celebrating. The neighborhood was noisy and full of life, the very thing I liked about it. Directly across the canal at Arnie's, some spicy seafood was grilling. I was hyper-conscious of each breath I took in and let out.

I had no idea what my life would look like from the next week on. I'd thought about where to go but made no arrangements. I had girlfriends who would welcome me, though most of them were busy with husbands and young kids. I could go back home to Philadelphia and my parents' house for a short time. They would accept my explanation that I had to leave Jack. That he had a temper and it got bad. They wouldn't probe for details. That wasn't their way. I could sleep in my twin bed until noon, as long as I could put up with the disapproving looks I'd get from my mother—a lifelong early riser. I could go up to Ithaca to stay with Doris and Joe and play with my young nieces. Right before the opening of school, I could rent a place on the North Shore close to my job.

The mimosa, with its graceful draping branches created a haven for me, but I had to get back inside to finish preparing dinner. The picnic table wasn't set, and the lasagna needed warming. While the oven heated up, I spooned the clam stuffing onto the shells and positioned them on baking sheets. As I did, my heart fluttered, sending a chill down to my toes. *Oh, yes, the holiday's almost over. It's happening. I'm leaving.* My heart sank. I singled out six of the biggest shells full of stuffing, added two more, and set them on a plate that I wrapped in plastic. I wedged that plate of clams carefully into the freezer, for Jack to heat up after I'd gone.

52.

On the holiday Monday I read an entire book, though I have no idea which one it was. I was on hyper-alert the whole day fearing that Jack wouldn't be out of the house long enough for me to call Maxine and make sure I could stay with her.

On Tuesday I found a way to calm myself by accepting that without any set of instructions to follow, no book to tell me how to leave a husband, I would have to do whatever I felt was right. I ran errands and called Maxine from a phone booth. I bought groceries to stack on the shelves and stuff in the freezer. I went to the bank where we had separate accounts. I took four hundred dollars from mine and deposited it into Jack's to even them out. I returned library books.

On Wednesday I got my suitcase down from a closet, filled it without much thought and slid it under the bed. I canceled appointments. I paid bills. I watered plants. I decided what to wear the next day and what to bury in my purse. I slipped on the opal ring with diamond chips from my Aunt Helen, my only piece of expensive jewelry, in case I would never again see the things I left behind. For dinner I cooked enough pasta to generate leftovers. I didn't feel scared. I didn't feel nervous. I was a machine performing a series of pre-programmed tasks.

Then early on Thursday morning I drove to the post office to fill out a hold-mail form. When I tried to start my car back up in the parking lot, I turned the key and nothing happened. Dead. "This *cannot* happen today," I shouted at the universe. I sat and waited, then tried it again. Nothing. I twisted the key hard five more times, more angry than hopeful. Silence. Back inside, I used their phone to call Jack.

"I'm down at the post office. My car's not turning over at all. I've tried it a bunch of times. Can you come over and get me?"

"What are you doing over there?"

"Getting stamps." It was not a complete lie.

"Geez, it's probably the starter. I doubt I can fix it but I'll be over."

We waited together for the tow truck. On the way home, I practiced this sentence again and again before I finally said, "I have my session this afternoon—"

"Do you want the van?"

"No, I don't want to deal with parking in the city. I'll check the schedule and take the train." I spoke as though they were my lines in a play. "Can you drive me to the station?"

An hour later the owner of the service station called us at home and delivered the news—it was a faulty ignition switch, and the needed part wouldn't come in until the beginning of the following week.

The bad news rolled right over me. The quiet voice inside me was my guide. Nothing would stop me from doing what I'd promised myself I'd do. I could have waited until my car was fixed so I could stash my filled suitcase in the trunk. But I was prepared to leave with nothing but the clothes on my back and whatever would fit in my handbag. And I certainly wasn't going to hang around wondering if my car's breakdown was a sign.

That afternoon I couldn't sit down. My feet kept moving, and my hands fingered every surface and object in the house. Mid-afternoon I called outside, "It's time to go, Jack." I stood back so he couldn't see my trembling lips. Walking out to the car I looked at my feet so I wouldn't have to bear seeing one of the cats.

Jack pulled the van into the station parking lot near the platform for city-bound trains. As I got out I turned to him and, with the bright afternoon sun blinding me, said, "Thanks. Bye." I closed the car door and, out of the corner of my eye, I saw him drive away.

I was full of feelings, I know now, but I had buried them deep enough to keep them unearthed until it was safe. If they had risen up at that moment, I might have crumpled right onto the concrete parking lot.

Sitting in Carl's waiting room, I had time to think about what I was going to tell him. How controlled I was, I think now, that I didn't want to run in and scream, "I left Jack!" I have to assume my hesitation came from questioning whether I was sure I'd really go through with it. I'd picked up Carl's frustration with me—my empowered talk in therapy that I didn't follow through on. How many times had he heard me say, "I'm not going to take it anymore"? I was sure I'd do it, but I wanted to tell him afterwards that I had done it. So at my session that Thursday I talked about the end of the school year and details of the weekend with Jack's family. I wasn't tempted to tell him; I wanted to do this alone.

After my session, out in the hot evening air on 57ᵗʰ Street, I hesitated in front of his office, especially aware of my feet planted on the sidewalk. I could feel strength building in my chest. *I can do it; I'm sure. I'm not going home.*

I found a public phone and called Maxine. "Okay to come out now for a couple of days? I'm going to do it."

"Sure. Sure. Come on out. We're here."

"Thank you, thank—"

"Are you safe now? Where are you?"

"On my way to Penn Station. I was at therapy. I can take a train that'll get me there around 7:40."

"I'll get the room ready and pick you up at the station."

Walking downtown I was confident that Maxine's house was the right place for me, and her husband Sid was the major reason. Jack knew him as one of the leaders of the county teachers' union and respected him. Sid was strong-willed, articulate, and loud—the kind of union representative that doesn't take shit from anyone. In other words, just the kind of person I wanted to be around that night. I paced down to Penn Station, all twenty-plus blocks, stopping only for a slice of pizza.

As soon as I stepped into their house, they both hugged me tightly. That's what I needed from them—hugs, not questions, not talk. When I followed them into the kitchen and saw the phone I stiffened, thinking about how it was time to do the scariest thing I'd ever done in my life—tell Jack our marriage was over.

I didn't have any plan for what I was going to say, but touching the phone put me into an automatic pilot mode. I dialed our home number and dropped onto a chair. It rang five or six times. I figured he must be outside, but then the receiver clicked and I heard, "Hello?"

He knew something was up I could tell. I wasn't home at my regular time.

"I'm out at Maxine's house," I said and grabbed a breath before I went on. She and Sid were in the other room, but I sensed them surrounding me. "I'm staying here tonight and for a couple more nights until I decide where to go next." That's the only way I could get it out. I could never have uttered the words, "I'm leaving you."

He was silent for a few seconds, but then his words came at me like pellets. "Don't do this," he said. "Don't do this. Please. Don't do this."

I'd prepared myself for anger, for manipulation, for threats. I'd imagined all the things he might say and told myself to remember I was safe; they were nothing but words. Yet there was only panic in his voice.

"I have to," I said staring at the floor. The words were coming out easily. The terror in his voice told me he understood this was the end. "I have to," I said again, mostly for myself.

After a few minutes of repeating ourselves, I handed the phone over to Sid to talk Jack out of coming to their house. I heard Sid say with the authority of a black-robed judge, "It's over, man."

53.

I don't remember sadness or fear after calling Jack. I remember a flood of relief and then a fatigue that felt more like the complete physical exhaustion one must feel after climbing Kilimanjaro. Maxine and I, who at school would gab for hours, just exchanged short clips about necessities. Towel? Soap? Breakfast? There was nothing more to be said.

Once Sid's untrained guard dogs, two especially large German Shepherds, got comfortable with me and I with them, I settled into the room that would be my home for the next few days. As I undressed and put on the nightshirt Maxine lent me, I realized how lucky I was to have found people who were not afraid of conflict. They were confident and brave and in control. As much as I loved my parents, they simply were not up to this job. I crawled into the bed and sleep found me right away.

The next morning I took out a pocket notebook I'd just bought and started the journal practice I still follow. The first page had only one sentence: "I can't believe I did it." The phone rang on the other side of my wall, and I could tell that Sid was talking to Jack. In less than a minute I heard the receiver click down.

"Jack called," Sid told me when I went into the kitchen for breakfast. "I told him you won't speak to him for the next few days. He said he wouldn't call again 'til you want to talk to him."

That wasn't like Jack to cave in so easily. Sid was strong and loud but he wasn't frightening and didn't have a gun. The only thing that made sense to me about Jack's behavior was that my leaving was not a surprise to him. He must have felt the growing power in me and my burgeoning will to take care of myself.

"How are you doing?" Maxine said as she scrambled some eggs.

"Okay," I said, "Really, I feel surprisingly okay. I'm not sure where I'll go next, but I know I need to find a place to stay for a while."

"Use the phone to make your calls whenever you want."

Over the next two days I let the most important people in my life know what was going on. I called my sister and my mother, asking her to tell Aunt Helen. I called Carl and left a message on his machine to let him know and to cancel my next few appointments. I called Lynn and Carrie, friends who felt like family. Carrie invited me to stay with her family at their summerhouse upstate for as long as I needed after leaving Maxine's.

On my fourth morning in Maxine's spare bedroom, I woke up with a surprising clarity. The numbness was waning. I did it. I did what I had to do, and I was proud. After breakfast I checked in with the service station and learned the car would be ready by the end of the day. I called Jack.

"My car's fixed and I'm going to pick it up tomorrow mid-morning," I said business-like. "I want to come by with Maxine and pack up a few bags of clothes and things. You have to be someplace else." I sounded sure and strong to myself.

He didn't say anything right away. "Are you sure you want to do this?"

"Yes. Yes I am." When I heard the sadness in his voice, I was thankful I wasn't looking at his face or standing close enough to hug him.

"I can't stop you," he said as if talking to himself. "I'll go out and leave the back door unlocked."

I had prayed this conversation would not evolve into an ordeal, and I was surprised at how it was going. It was so unlike the Jack I'd been married to for five years. *Someone's helping him* flashed across my mind.

The next morning Maxine drove me to the service station, and then we caravanned to the house. When I pulled up in front, I felt a cold wave wash over me. It looked different to me already—smaller, more tired. Jack would have called the yard lush, but I saw it as stuffed and overgrown. The early summer perennials were starting to bloom. As I got out of the car, I noticed the scarlet canna we'd ordered the year before looked as good as the picture in the catalog.

I led Maxine toward the back deck where Jack had left the door unlocked. From the far corner of the backyard, Isaac and Isabelle came meowing toward me. I crouched down on the flagstone to let them rub against me, and I broke into deep, gasping sobs, the first time I'd cried since I left.

That made it real. I was a visitor. I didn't live there anymore.

54.

How do you say thank you to someone who helps you as Maxine and Sid had helped me? On the steamy morning I left their house, I put my suitcase in my car and went back to their front door. I hugged each one and said, "Thank you so, so much," as if they had just served me a delicious meal. It didn't feel right even then, but I didn't know what else to do. Besides, I knew Maxine and I would have plenty of time to chew it all over later.

That hot July day I headed off the Island and north toward Carrie's summer place in the country. I sped along the Henry Hudson Parkway in my VW with the front windows open and my hair swirling around me like Janis Joplin's. I had *Hotel California*, my favorite album, on the eight-track and sang along especially loudly when the Eagles ended with, "Maybe someday we will find, it wasn't really wasted time."

I felt raw, but joyfully raw. I was a different person already, stunningly aware that every speck of my mental energy could go into my day, my week, my life. The vortex that was Jack had been sucking my allotment of energy into its mass. The distance I had put between the two of us already had worked like a transfusion.

In those first days of separation I experienced only a complete relief. I was exhausted from the life I'd been living. I didn't have a millisecond of regret that I had left. It was brilliantly clear to me that my very being had been at stake.

I was exhilarated by the idea that my world now consisted simply of me and my little car. And as far as I knew, I had everything that I would ever have from my marriage in its trunk.

As I sped along the highway, a sporty dark car pulled up alongside me. I didn't normally notice what kind of cars were around me, but that one was staying right next to me, matching my speed. The person in the passenger seat rolled down his window all the way so I could see that he was a good-looking guy in a wide-striped rugby shirt. *Oh no,* I thought, *a flat tire? Broken tailpipe?* But he was laughing, turning to the driver, then back to me yelling something in a playful way.

"What?" I gestured with raised shoulders; I didn't have the kind of looks that stopped men in their tracks. He pointed ahead towards the right. I could make out only the word "Exit."

I stuck my left hand out the window. "I can't," I yelled, wiggling the gold ring I was still wearing. "I'm married."

I was puzzled by my reaction—hiding behind my wedding ring when I had just become unmarried? But my behavior in the months that followed showed how unready I was to be a single, available woman. Most of that time when I was around the opposite sex, I felt as naked as a deer in the woods trying to avoid a man with a gun.

Two weeks later, I drove back down the Henry Hudson Parkway, renewed after spending time with my friend and her family. I'd often forgotten that I was a person who had just left her marriage. I swam in the lake, helped her make salads, sang along endlessly to *The Wizard of Oz* with her little girl, and when I wanted, I stayed by myself. Carrie and I didn't talk much about my leaving. It was done and didn't come as much of a surprise to her. Like other people close to me, she may not have known exactly what was going on but had noticed I'd become a diminished version of myself.

Getting on with my life was what filled my mind as I neared Manhattan. I had an exciting plan; Carrie had offered me her empty Upper West Side apartment for as long as I needed while she and her family were away. Nothing could have been better.

I settled in and woke up each morning eager to get out onto the city streets and do errands, mostly for things I hadn't thought to pick up when I'd gone back to the house with Maxine. I took the elevator down the eleven floors each morning and walked the streets as though I were a tourist from Kansas taking it all in for the first time. One day I walked down to Lincoln Center and sat by the fountain, imagining every slim, erect woman who passed to be a dancer and every barrel-chested woman, a diva. Another day I walked into Central Park past the Tavern on the Green, wondering if any famous authors or actors were having lunch inside. I strolled over to Rockefeller Center, a must-see spot on my childhood trips to Manhattan. I had begged my parents each time to go into the imposing office building by the statue of Atlas and see my paternal grandfather's name still listed in the lobby directory from a business he no longer ran. Seeing his name—my name—permanently part of that city gave me a thrill that lasted, it appears, for a lifetime.

Mostly, though, I walked the streets imagining how much I'd love to live in Manhattan. Which was better—an apartment in a brownstone or in a high-rise? Maybe one with a little balcony? But the East Side was probably more convenient for my commute. It was so easy to dream big on those city streets.

One day, a young man with long dirty hair stood on the corner of Broadway and 72nd passing out blue flyers to any female who would take one from him. In those days, I felt responsible to take any handout offered to me so the person's feelings wouldn't be hurt. Lower mortgage rates? New Off-Broadway play? It didn't matter. I took the sheets home and promptly threw them away.

This guy was giving out notices about free pregnancy tests, with a consultation afterwards, at a place somewhere in the neighborhood. It was only three years after Roe v. Wade had been decided and, for the first time, "pregnancy" and "choices" were being used openly in the same sentence. I glanced quickly at the flyer and as usual stuffed it in my purse.

I didn't throw the blue flyer away that night though. I looked at it again, folded it and put it back in my bag. Usually I could count on my period being as regular as a woman's could be, twenty-eight days on the dot, but this month it hadn't come on the day I'd expected it. Actually, I couldn't remember when my next one was due. I wasn't worrying; after all, I'd just gone through the most stressful time of my life, and three years of infertility made it easy to discount a possible pregnancy.

If that test hadn't been free or close by, I don't think I would have gone to the address on the flyer. But as the building was only a few blocks away I did, "To rule it out," as a doctor might say. I rang the bell at the nondescript storefront door and got buzzed in. I checked in with a young woman in a white uniform, filled out a form, turned in my urine sample, and made an appointment to come back for the results.

55.

On the day I returned to the clinic, a soft-spoken young woman asked me to sit down at her desk. We exchanged pleasantries, but I felt my lips tightening in confusion. I'd expected to simply be given a sheet of paper.

"Your test was positive," she said, reaching for a notebook on her desk. A smile began in my heart, but then I gulped as I took in the meaning of her words. "You'll need to think about what you might do now," she said quietly.

"I threw away half of the Clomid," I said to her with no explanation. "Are you absolutely sure?"

"Yes, I am sure."

I sat in cold silence, struck by how alone I was at that moment. Not just staying-in-a-big-apartment-by-myself alone, but cosmically alone.

"Do you need some time to think it over?"

Think? I couldn't do anything as normal as think. Every cell in my brain had something to say, but I must've appeared comatose to her as I stared through a diploma on the wall.

After a respectful pause she added, "Are you going to bring the father in on this?"

Leaving the clinic, I turned onto Broadway and marched along with no idea where I was going. I couldn't stop my feet from accelerating down that street even if I had wanted to. At the light, shoulders and elbows and handbags knocked into me from every direction. "Get away from me!" I wanted to scream. I pivoted sharply onto an empty side street that wound through the short blocks of the neighborhood and traipsed, eyes down, without any sense of time. My head was filled with one cry: *I can't go back. I can't go back. I can't go back.* "Go back" didn't mean to me just getting in the car, driving to the house, telling Jack I was pregnant, bringing in my suitcase, and putting my toothbrush back in the holder. "Go back" meant plunging into that deep, dark place inside me that had been filled with shame and terror and guilt and heartbreak. Now that I'd been spending time by myself, I could see the price I'd paid for living in a place where I had to shut down and deny myself the chance to discover who I was and who I could be.

If I had known even one woman then who was single, raising a child, and working full-time as a teacher, I might have considered that life. But I didn't, so it didn't emerge as an option for me. Being pregnant meant only one thing: If I had a baby I would have to go back to Jack. All I could think was, *I can't go back . . . I won't go back . . . I can't let this seed grow.* I rushed back to the lab office that afternoon, not for a consultation but for a referral. I called one of the numbers they gave me and made an appointment for the end of the week at a reputable clinic that bore the name of a women's rights activist. The secretary who helped me said the process would take a few hours for an intake interview, the procedure, and recovery.

56.

On the scheduled day I took the subway downtown, though I'd been told I would need to take a cab back. "Have a seat along the wall on your left," the woman at the sign-in desk said. "We'll call you when the in-take counselor is ready."

I settled into my seat along what I assumed was the "before" wall. The others in my row had someone sitting with them. A young woman whispered to a guy she sat with, and a teenager fingered through a magazine while a middle-aged woman waited next to her. Carrie was the only person I had told what I was doing, but when she offered to come with me, I told her no I'd be fine. I could handle it. I was sure I was doing the right thing. I was being that little soldier who'd taught herself well how to be alone.

In the row of seats across from me, a young woman sat with her eyes closed and her head on a friend's shoulder. I imagined that was the "after" wall. I willed myself to breathe.

Then I heard my name, jumped up, and followed an assistant into the in-take counselor's office. I was surprised that she was so young, but she smiled warmly as she motioned for me to sit across from her and asked if I wanted some water. Her first questions covered physical information. Last period? Spotting? Pain? Doctor's name? But then her questions lead to other things. "Why do you want to terminate this pregnancy?"

The words tumbled out as I told her how I'd just left my husband after living with him for over five years and putting up with his frightening anger and physical abuse. How I'd been working with a fertility specialist because I wanted to have children someday, and I wanted to find out why I couldn't get pregnant. I laid out all my confused behavior in front of this young woman who looked directly into my eyes, glancing down only to take notes.

"I wanted to leave him for so long but it was so hard to do. He'd been brought up in a house with a lot of abuse. It was all he knew." I hesitated; I was ashamed of how naïve or stupid this next thing would sound. "I never thought a few pills would work. I didn't even take the full regimen. I didn't want to be pregnant now. I only wanted to find out what's wrong with me."

I left nothing out as I talked. She listened and wrote and didn't judge. I understand now that such a counselor might often hear young women reporting behavior, as mine did, that goes against all common sense.

The next minutes occurred in slow motion. After the in-take session, she directs me to a dressing room where I take off my clothes and slip on a cotton gown. A nurse leads me to a room where the procedure is to be done. I climb onto the table and sit between the stirrups while she introduces me to the other nurse. The doctor swings the door open and walks in. He's a tall, forty-something man, with curly dark hair and an Italian last name. The nurse helps me lie back on the table while the doctor looks at my chart. I'm hoping for immediate sedation or anything to dull my awareness of where I am and what's happening, but no one budges. I try to rub some warmth into my hands.

After a minute the doctor stops reading and looks up at the nurse.

"I'm not going to do it," he says as if it's all one word. She looks at him grimly, waiting for an explanation.

"I can't do it with this history," he says, lifting my chart. "Fertility pills?"

I struggle to sit up. The nurse helps me.

"No, please," I say to no one special. "I can't have a baby now. I finally left. It was a really bad situation."

He's facing me now. "With what I'm reading here, you'll have to meet with an on-staff social worker before I'd consider it."

"Of course, of course, I'll do that."

The doctor nods good-bye to the others and shuts the door solidly.

I turn to the head nurse. "Can I get dressed now and see the social worker?"

"I'm so sorry," she says. "No social workers are here on Friday afternoons. We can get you in to see her on Monday." She rubs my arm. "I'm really sorry."

So that afternoon I climbed down from the table, got dressed, walked back out into the waiting room and sat along the "before" wall for the fifteen minutes they'd requested. I slinked out the door and took the subway back to the apartment, now that I didn't need to call a cab.

Looking out Carrie's living-room window, I stared at the streets buzzing with activity. People zipped along the sidewalks, evidently intent on beginning weekend plans. Cars zoomed along Westside Highway, and a tour boat drifted up the Hudson. All the same, it felt like the loneliest place in the world. There was no way I could stand actually being alone. There was only one place I could think of going.

As soon as my Aunt Helen picked up the receiver, I started talking. "I've got something really big going on, and I don't want to be alone this weekend. I'm not ready to talk about it now, but I will sometime. I badly need peace and quiet . . . oh, and lots of sleep. Can I come stay with you?"

"Of course," she said. "I'm glad you called me."

I must have slept most of the weekend; I remember little, only a gigantic headache. Aunt Helen gave me aspirins, made me tea, and let me take over her only bedroom. I must have been overwrought with battling emotions—anger that I had been turned away, fear and anxiety about what was to come next, and a deep heavy sadness about it all.

Back in New York on Monday morning I got to my appointment with the social worker early. I checked in and began sorting through the magazines when I heard my name called. A tall woman in a business suit motioned for me to come with her, and we took seats across from each other at the desk in her office. I started talking right away, but she interrupted.

"Listen, I've read everything in your file," she said. "Why don't we just take you in for the procedure right now, and we can talk afterwards." So we walked down the hall where a nurse guided me into a room, and twenty minutes later, it was over. I took a cab back to the apartment, and before the long night's sleep that followed, I promised myself I would plan the rest of my life in the morning.

57.

During the months that followed, I lived in two distinct realities. One was my everyday life where I felt giddy with optimism about the new life I was building. It's the reality I remember most; it's the easiest to relive. Throughout the summer I spent my time with friends and family. When I told them Jack had been physically abusive, no one appeared shocked, and I was pleased that no one asked for details. As the summer wound down, I found a cheap, makeshift apartment in a house near my work. By the time school started in late August, I was full of energy and optimism. Within a month I started hanging out with two single women at my school.

The journal I kept reminds me of the other reality I lived in, the one that enveloped me during the quiet times. Alone at night I scribbled on and on in my notebook, letting out such raw emotion that the scrawl is unrecognizable to me now. *Will I get to have kids someday? Will I be this lonely for the rest of my life? Will I ever stop missing Jack?*

I was in that darker world too during therapy. There anger burst out of me, mainly at myself: *Why did I stay with such an angry man? How could I let him do those things to me? What the hell was I thinking when I had the affair?*

In January, six months after leaving the marriage, I saw Jack for the first time. It must have started with a phone call, though I'm not sure. He told me that on the day after I left, he had started working with Michael the therapist whose card he kept from our time in sex therapy. After that, Jack and I probably called each other more frequently, and then maybe I went over to talk, lingering there and soaking in the comfort of that little house and the dear cats who brushed between and around my legs over and over. Jack told me what his sisters and brothers were up to and how the new wrestling season was going. I told him about my teeny studio apartment that had no kitchen, just a shelf next to the toilet with a hot plate on it. We both talked about what we were working on in therapy. One night I stayed over, and then I stayed over the next weekend too, and then for a couple more weekends. It probably goes without saying that we started having sex again.

One Sunday his family came over to the house. I burst out crying as they walked in, and I couldn't stop sobbing until my stomach hurt too much to bear. I went back to my apartment early that day.

I sensed that the tears I'd shed hadn't come from joy at the idea of reuniting. They came from somewhere more honest. They were whispers from the voice I'd been learning to follow, the knowing voice deep inside me that said, *Don't do it. You're not ready. He's not ready. Stay where you are. Keep doing what you're doing.* And sadly, I once again had to tell Jack I was leaving him. I understand now that the time and emotional space I gave myself to heal and grow was the kindest thing I could have done for myself. Maybe for Jack, too.

58.

For the next two years we simply lived our lives and considered ourselves separated. I saw Carl regularly, and I heard from a friend that Jack continued to work with his psychologist. Neither of us had the resolve to make our separation legal or to divorce. I suppose that says something about the strong connection we'd had.

By the time Jack and I got around to finalizing things legally, in 1979, I had a studio apartment in Manhattan, living the dream I'd had since childhood. I was finally able to afford a place in the city thanks to a subsidized-rent program. I had an hour commute out to Heritage and kept WNEW on nonstop. The apartment was only a quarter of the size of my first apartment with Lynn on Long Island, but it was on the 27th floor of a high rise and, as I saw it, pretty close to heaven. The wall of windows exposed the East River and hundreds of apartments that I peered at, imagining the stories within. I told myself regularly it wouldn't be so bad if I never married. I could live out the rest of my life in this city, going anywhere and doing anything I wanted.

Jack initiated the divorce in '79, three summers after we separated, since he wanted to marry the woman he'd been seeing. Since she was an attorney, we agreed to have her write up our divorce papers. With no children and few possessions, our settlement was straightforward and equitable.

To sign the divorce papers, he and I met at a restaurant near my uptown apartment in the middle of a July afternoon. It's a scene I'll forever carry with me. We sat across from each other at a small table near the empty bar, with a glass of wine at each place. We chatted as though we were old school friends at a reunion. I bombarded him with questions about his family, the cats, and the woman he was about to marry.

"I'm happy for you, Jack. That you found a good woman."

"Thanks. You'd like her, I think. What about you? You have anyone?"

"Not now. I was dating a teacher from school last year, but I broke it off. He has a lot of baggage; I couldn't see myself married to him. We had fun together though." (That was my shorthand for sex, vodka, and rock and roll.) "Nice guy . . . a great dancer, too," I said.

Jack laughed. "You always liked to dance."

"Sure do. I'm taking tap dancing at the 92nd Street Y now." I took a sip of wine while I rested in the pleasure of how good that felt to say. "I'd like to find someone soon, though."

After signing all the papers, I put down the pen. There was one thing I needed to find out before we parted. I swallowed awkwardly, gathering my nerve. "Can I ask you something?"

"Sure. What?"

I took a deep breath and leaned in to whisper, "You don't hit her, do you?"

"Oh, my God, no," he gulped. His face reddened and he blinked sharply. "Oh, God, Betty. I can't believe . . . I am so, so sorry." I grabbed his hand and held it tightly. The two of us sat like that in the empty restaurant for a long time, our hands clasped across the table and our faces washed with tears.

Epilogue

December 2015

As I was writing this book, I searched for photos taken during the years I spent with Jack to help me bring them alive. But of the hundreds of pictures I took during our time together, I have with me now only one little yellow box of Kodak slides with "Memorial Day '76" scribbled across it in my handwriting. I've carried that container of slides with me in the bottom of a carton for decades as I moved from house to house, state to state with my husband and son.

Those slides, from that holiday weekend two months before I left Jack, reveal his family at a cookout in our backyard. It must have been a chilly holiday that year; we're all wearing heavy sweaters or jackets.

When I slipped the first slide into the hand-held viewer and held it up to my eyes, I gasped. I felt as though I had jumped back all those decades onto the hard sand of the backyard with the railroad ties framing the rich, black soil of the flowerbeds. Smiling at me are Jack's brother Brian and sister Diane, who's wearing pigtails that day.

One by one I slipped the slides in. The backyard looks so small. Everything is on display—the sheltering mimosa tree, the gardens already filling, and the two boats docked alongside the bulkhead. The canal glistens, reminding me how I never tired of watching the ebb and flow of the tides. There's a faded green hose strung out in haphazard loops across the sand and a shovel leaning against a bench. Other pictures show how messy the yard is with things that were part

215

of Jack's botanical projects—homemade screens sheltering seedlings and plastic pipes rigged up to support early flowers.

I could see we were roasting marshmallows on the Hibachi that day. In one picture someone must have just handled me a stick with a burnt marshmallow on it. My twisted face shows that it has just gone into my mouth, and I'm struggling with the burning goop that has exploded with my first bite. I'm looking at the photographer (Jack, I assume), not happy with him or the fire in my mouth. I look tired, worn out. I think now I can read something else in my look—anguish that I kept hidden in those months when I knew that I must take care of myself and leave, no matter how hard it was going to be.

The next slide from that roll of film shows Jack inside the house. Memorial Day must have passed. His face is sunburned, and he's wearing short sleeves. I immediately recalled the moment I took that picture, after running to my room for my camera to capture something that had made me laugh.

In this picture Jack is leaning toward me with his right elbow on the end of the butcher-block slab that dominated our kitchen. His bright red cheeks and sunburned nose show he's had a day out in the sun. He's wearing a white T-shirt with the Budweiser logo he used to wear in his first apartment in Bayside. His face shows pure bliss.

The table displays the reason for his happiness. Lying on their sides in a neat row are eight large striped bass, each almost as long as the width of the table. Right between the third and fourth fish is his glass of red wine, half empty, with slimy fish scales pressed on its stem. Just inches away sits a plastic container of worms, also half empty. Down at Jack's foot is the open cooler that carried home his quarry, the one I remember for its smell of chum and fish entrails and beer.

In the foreground two feline ears pop up into camera range. It's Isaac who had jumped up onto a kitchen stool to check out the bounty. He's sitting at attention. Jack looks like he doesn't have a care in the world—a boatload of fish plopped on the table, some worms for tomorrow, a cat nearby, a glass of wine, and me there, laughing along with him.

When I found only this one box of slides, I was surprised, but I understand now. All the other pictures remained in our house that July, stashed away in bags and boxes where I couldn't get to them quickly when I went back with Maxine to pack up. I'd stuffed my Nikon into my pocketbook the day I left, and these were still in the camera—this last picture from the Fourth of July weekend.

Jack appears again in one of my photo albums, among shots documenting the life I built in New York City after leaving our marriage. There's only the one photo of him in the middle of pictures from vacations I took with girlfriends to the Caribbean, a semester-abroad program I ran in France, and visits with my sister and her growing family.

It's labeled "Aug. '79," and it was taken on the last day I ever saw him. He had called me to ask if he could bring his new wife into the city to meet me. In the photo, Jack is sitting on my couch, grinning broadly at the camera and holding my orange cat Romeo in a tight hug. Jack's right leg is folded on the couch exposing an Ace bandage wrapped around his ankle, probably the result of one of the messy house renovations he'd told me about. Leaning into him, sporting a wide grin that combines pride and relief about the easy atmosphere in my place is his new wife. She looks younger than her twenty-nine years. Her wavy brown hair is parted with barrettes holding back her bangs.

For all I know Jack might also have a picture of me from that day. I would imagine that in it I might be sitting on my couch with either Romeo or fluffy little Gloria padding across my lap, with a strong color on my cheeks—not from the tropics, but from the active, outdoor life I'm living in the city. Or maybe Jack would have posed me next to my easel that held a wet painting of a nude. Without a doubt, I would have a broad smile across my face.

Things were ending well. And things were beginning.

Questions for Readers

1. Do you think Betty's family life affected her choice of a husband and her view of marriage?

2. Were there any details she includes that brought the '70s alive for you?

3. Were you as surprised as young Betty was when Jack first struck her?

4. Since Betty is telling the story, do you think she minimizes her role in their troubled dynamics?

5. What does the title *Not Exactly Love* mean to you?

6. What passages strike you as insightful?

7. How does Betty change or mature by the end of the book?

8. Do you approve or disapprove of her choices?

9. If you could ask Betty one question, what would it be?

10. Has this memoir broadened your perspective in any way?

Acknowledgments

Thanks to Brooke Warner, Cait Levin and the team at She Writes Press for their efforts to bring women's stories like mine out into the world. And special thanks to my She Writes sisters who generously share their experiences and wisdom.

Thanks especially to three people whose encouragement and feedback over the last five years were key to the development of this book—Carrie Carmichael, Paula Schuster, and Marge Rachlen. Special thanks also to editors Lizzie Skurnick and Barbara Esstman who helped shape my memories into a story and Eva Zimmerman who helped get this book out into the world.

Thanks to the Southampton Writers Conference for its joyful, inspiring atmosphere and the wonderful workshops I took with Mary Karr, Melissa Banks, Matthew Klam, and Kaylie Jones.

Thanks to my readers, Suzanne Finney, Susan Miller Souers, Carol Walsh, Dori Hambleton, Kim Ketner, Stephen Sinclair, Nicol Cole, Len Lapidus, and to the many classmates at The Writer's Center in Bethesda, MD and the Southampton Writers Conference whose feedback helped immeasurably. I also want to thank Maureen Green for sharing this book with Laurie Duker and Judy Whiton of Court Watch Montgomery.

Thanks go also to my familial sisterhood for the affection and joy I get from them: Dori, Marcia, Kim, Karen, Carolyn, Jan, and Ginny. And lastly thanks to my three guys, Will, Pete, and the ever-cuddly Augie who show me love and support in their own special ways.

About the Author

© Carol K. Walsh

Betty Hafner has written monthly book reviews for more than a decade in *The Town Courier* newspaper in Montgomery County, MD. She wrote two practical career-change books that stemmed from her workshops for adults—*Where Do I Go From Here?* published by Lippincott (2001) and *The Nurse's Guide to Starting a Small Business*, published by Pilot Books (1992). With an MS in counseling, Hafner considers herself a teacher and counselor by trade and by nature, but she also loves telling stories through her artwork, photographs, and writing. She lives outside Washington, DC with her husband.